T0336495

THIS IS YOUR **PASSBOOK**® FOR ...

FARE ENFORCEMENT AGENT

NATIONAL LEARNING CORPORATION®
passbooks.com

PASSBOOK® SERIES

THE *PASSBOOK® SERIES* has been created to prepare applicants and candidates for the ultimate academic battlefield – the examination room.

At some time in our lives, each and every one of us may be required to take an examination – for validation, matriculation, admission, qualification, registration, certification, or licensure.

Based on the assumption that every applicant or candidate has met the basic formal educational standards, has taken the required number of courses, and read the necessary texts, the *PASSBOOK® SERIES* furnishes the one special preparation which may assure passing with confidence, instead of failing with insecurity. Examination questions – together with answers – are furnished as the basic vehicle for study so that the mysteries of the examination and its compounding difficulties may be eliminated or diminished by a sure method.

This book is meant to help you pass your examination provided that you qualify and are serious in your objective.

The entire field is reviewed through the huge store of content information which is succinctly presented through a provocative and challenging approach – the question-and-answer method.

A climate of success is established by furnishing the correct answers at the end of each test.

You soon learn to recognize types of questions, forms of questions, and patterns of questioning. You may even begin to anticipate expected outcomes.

You perceive that many questions are repeated or adapted so that you can gain acute insights, which may enable you to score many sure points.

You learn how to confront new questions, or types of questions, and to attack them confidently and work out the correct answers.

You note objectives and emphases, and recognize pitfalls and dangers, so that you may make positive educational adjustments.

Moreover, you are kept fully informed in relation to new concepts, methods, practices, and directions in the field.

You discover that you arre actually taking the examination all the time: you are preparing for the examination by "taking" an examination, not by reading extraneous and/or supererogatory textbooks.

In short, this PASSBOOK®, used directedly, should be an important factor in helping you to pass your test.

FARE ENFORCEMENT AGENT

DUTIES
Fare Enforcement Agents, under supervision, perform surveillance, investigative and enforcement work to ensure passenger compliance with current fare policies of MTA Transit. They check the validity of customers' receipts on Transit revenue vehicles to ensure payment is made in accordance with existing fare policies; issue summonses to fare evaders and exercise resilience and de-escalation techniques with agitated customers who may have violated fare policy; investigate alleged violations of fare enforcement; participate in the monitoring and coordinating activities of team members and assist them as necessary; testify at hearings and in court regarding the details of summonses issued; provide route and fare-related information to customers, and assist and instruct them to use fare receipt issuance machines; record daily actions in memo books and prepare reports; perform special assignments as needed; operate a motor vehicle; and perform related work.

SCOPE OF THE EXAMINATION
The multiple-choice test may include questions that require the use of any of the following abilities:

Written Comprehension – The ability to understand written sentences and paragraphs. Example: Understanding written bulletins released by MTA Transit.

Written Expression – The ability to use English words or sentences in writing so others will understand. Example: Writing incident reports regarding unusual occurrences.

Problem Sensitivity – The ability to tell when something is wrong or is likely to go wrong. It includes being able to identify the whole problem as well as the elements of the problem. Example: Observing a person not paying their bus fare and recognizing it as a problem.

Deductive Reasoning – The ability to apply general rules to specific problems to come up with logical answers. It involves deciding if an answer makes sense. Example: Applying MTA Transit rules and regulations to situations to determine the appropriate action that must be taken.

Inductive Reasoning – The ability to combine separate pieces of information, or specific answers to problems, to form general rules or conclusions. It includes coming up with a logical explanation for why a series of unrelated events occur together. Example: Identifying a suspicious and/or unsafe situation based on different issues observed to form a conclusion about the incident.

Information Ordering – The ability to correctly follow a rule or set of rules to arrange things or actions in a certain order. The rule or sets of rules used must be given. The things or actions to be put in order can include numbers, letters, words, pictures, procedures, sentences, and mathematical or logical operations. Example: Following MTA Transit Rules and Regulations procedures in the correct order given.

Spatial Orientation – The ability to tell where you are in relation to the location of some object or to tell where the object is in relation to you. Example: Reading bus maps and determining the destination of the bus route.

Memorization – The ability to remember information, such as words, numbers, pictures and procedure. Example: Remembering details of a fare evasion incident on a bus.

Customer Service – The ability to work with customers to assess their needs, provide information or assistance, resolve their problems, or satisfy their expectations. Example: Providing travel directions to a customer.

HOW TO TAKE A TEST

I. YOU MUST PASS AN EXAMINATION

A. *WHAT EVERY CANDIDATE SHOULD KNOW*

Examination applicants often ask us for help in preparing for the written test. What can I study in advance? What kinds of questions will be asked? How will the test be given? How will the papers be graded?

As an applicant for a civil service examination, you may be wondering about some of these things. Our purpose here is to suggest effective methods of advance study and to describe civil service examinations.

Your chances for success on this examination can be increased if you know how to prepare. Those "pre-examination jitters" can be reduced if you know what to expect. You can even experience an adventure in good citizenship if you know why civil service exams are given.

B. *WHY ARE CIVIL SERVICE EXAMINATIONS GIVEN?*

Civil service examinations are important to you in two ways. As a citizen, you want public jobs filled by employees who know how to do their work. As a job seeker, you want a fair chance to compete for that job on an equal footing with other candidates. The best-known means of accomplishing this two-fold goal is the competitive examination.

Exams are widely publicized throughout the nation. They may be administered for jobs in federal, state, city, municipal, town or village governments or agencies.

Any citizen may apply, with some limitations, such as the age or residence of applicants. Your experience and education may be reviewed to see whether you meet the requirements for the particular examination. When these requirements exist, they are reasonable and applied consistently to all applicants. Thus, a competitive examination may cause you some uneasiness now, but it is your privilege and safeguard.

C. *HOW ARE CIVIL SERVICE EXAMS DEVELOPED?*

Examinations are carefully written by trained technicians who are specialists in the field known as "psychological measurement," in consultation with recognized authorities in the field of work that the test will cover. These experts recommend the subject matter areas or skills to be tested; only those knowledges or skills important to your success on the job are included. The most reliable books and source materials available are used as references. Together, the experts and technicians judge the difficulty level of the questions.

Test technicians know how to phrase questions so that the problem is clearly stated. Their ethics do not permit "trick" or "catch" questions. Questions may have been tried out on sample groups, or subjected to statistical analysis, to determine their usefulness.

Written tests are often used in combination with performance tests, ratings of training and experience, and oral interviews. All of these measures combine to form the best-known means of finding the right person for the right job.

II. HOW TO PASS THE WRITTEN TEST

A. NATURE OF THE EXAMINATION

To prepare intelligently for civil service examinations, you should know how they differ from school examinations you have taken. In school you were assigned certain definite pages to read or subjects to cover. The examination questions were quite detailed and usually emphasized memory. Civil service exams, on the other hand, try to discover your present ability to perform the duties of a position, plus your potentiality to learn these duties. In other words, a civil service exam attempts to predict how successful you will be. Questions cover such a broad area that they cannot be as minute and detailed as school exam questions.

In the public service similar kinds of work, or positions, are grouped together in one "class." This process is known as *position-classification*. All the positions in a class are paid according to the salary range for that class. One class title covers all of these positions, and they are all tested by the same examination.

B. FOUR BASIC STEPS

1) Study the announcement

How, then, can you know what subjects to study? Our best answer is: "Learn as much as possible about the class of positions for which you've applied." The exam will test the knowledge, skills and abilities needed to do the work.

Your most valuable source of information about the position you want is the official exam announcement. This announcement lists the training and experience qualifications. Check these standards and apply only if you come reasonably close to meeting them.

The brief description of the position in the examination announcement offers some clues to the subjects which will be tested. Think about the job itself. Review the duties in your mind. Can you perform them, or are there some in which you are rusty? Fill in the blank spots in your preparation.

Many jurisdictions preview the written test in the exam announcement by including a section called "Knowledge and Abilities Required," "Scope of the Examination," or some similar heading. Here you will find out specifically what fields will be tested.

2) Review your own background

Once you learn in general what the position is all about, and what you need to know to do the work, ask yourself which subjects you already know fairly well and which need improvement. You may wonder whether to concentrate on improving your strong areas or on building some background in your fields of weakness. When the announcement has specified "some knowledge" or "considerable knowledge," or has used adjectives like "beginning principles of..." or "advanced ... methods," you can get a clue as to the number and difficulty of questions to be asked in any given field. More questions, and hence broader coverage, would be included for those subjects which are more important in the work. Now weigh your strengths and weaknesses against the job requirements and prepare accordingly.

3) Determine the level of the position

Another way to tell how intensively you should prepare is to understand the level of the job for which you are applying. Is it the entering level? In other words, is this the position in which beginners in a field of work are hired? Or is it an intermediate or advanced level? Sometimes this is indicated by such words as "Junior" or "Senior" in the class title. Other jurisdictions use Roman numerals to designate the level – Clerk I, Clerk II, for example. The word "Supervisor" sometimes appears in the title. If the level is not indicated by the title, check the description of duties. Will you be working under very close supervision, or will you have responsibility for independent decisions in this work?

4) Choose appropriate study materials

Now that you know the subjects to be examined and the relative amount of each subject to be covered, you can choose suitable study materials. For beginning level jobs, or even advanced ones, if you have a pronounced weakness in some aspect of your training, read a modern, standard textbook in that field. Be sure it is up to date and has general coverage. Such books are normally available at your library, and the librarian will be glad to help you locate one. For entry-level positions, questions of appropriate difficulty are chosen – neither highly advanced questions, nor those too simple. Such questions require careful thought but not advanced training.

If the position for which you are applying is technical or advanced, you will read more advanced, specialized material. If you are already familiar with the basic principles of your field, elementary textbooks would waste your time. Concentrate on advanced textbooks and technical periodicals. Think through the concepts and review difficult problems in your field.

These are all general sources. You can get more ideas on your own initiative, following these leads. For example, training manuals and publications of the government agency which employs workers in your field can be useful, particularly for technical and professional positions. A letter or visit to the government department involved may result in more specific study suggestions, and certainly will provide you with a more definite idea of the exact nature of the position you are seeking.

III. KINDS OF TESTS

Tests are used for purposes other than measuring knowledge and ability to perform specified duties. For some positions, it is equally important to test ability to make adjustments to new situations or to profit from training. In others, basic mental abilities not dependent on information are essential. Questions which test these things may not appear as pertinent to the duties of the position as those which test for knowledge and information. Yet they are often highly important parts of a fair examination. For very general questions, it is almost impossible to help you direct your study efforts. What we can do is to point out some of the more common of these general abilities needed in public service positions and describe some typical questions.

1) General information

Broad, general information has been found useful for predicting job success in some kinds of work. This is tested in a variety of ways, from vocabulary lists to questions about current events. Basic background in some field of work, such as sociology or economics, may be sampled in a group of questions. Often these are principles which have become familiar to most persons through exposure rather than through formal training. It is difficult to advise you how to study for these questions; being alert to the world around you is our best suggestion.

2) Verbal ability

An example of an ability needed in many positions is verbal or language ability. Verbal ability is, in brief, the ability to use and understand words. Vocabulary and grammar tests are typical measures of this ability. Reading comprehension or paragraph interpretation questions are common in many kinds of civil service tests. You are given a paragraph of written material and asked to find its central meaning.

3) Numerical ability

Number skills can be tested by the familiar arithmetic problem, by checking paired lists of numbers to see which are alike and which are different, or by interpreting charts and graphs. In the latter test, a graph may be printed in the test booklet which you are asked to use as the basis for answering questions.

4) Observation

A popular test for law-enforcement positions is the observation test. A picture is shown to you for several minutes, then taken away. Questions about the picture test your ability to observe both details and larger elements.

5) Following directions

In many positions in the public service, the employee must be able to carry out written instructions dependably and accurately. You may be given a chart with several columns, each column listing a variety of information. The questions require you to carry out directions involving the information given in the chart.

6) Skills and aptitudes

Performance tests effectively measure some manual skills and aptitudes. When the skill is one in which you are trained, such as typing or shorthand, you can practice. These tests are often very much like those given in business school or high school courses. For many of the other skills and aptitudes, however, no short-time preparation can be made. Skills and abilities natural to you or that you have developed throughout your lifetime are being tested.

Many of the general questions just described provide all the data needed to answer the questions and ask you to use your reasoning ability to find the answers. Your best preparation for these tests, as well as for tests of facts and ideas, is to be at your physical and mental best. You, no doubt, have your own methods of getting into an exam-taking mood and keeping "in shape." The next section lists some ideas on this subject.

IV. KINDS OF QUESTIONS

Only rarely is the "essay" question, which you answer in narrative form, used in civil service tests. Civil service tests are usually of the short-answer type. Full instructions for answering these questions will be given to you at the examination. But in case this is your first experience with short-answer questions and separate answer sheets, here is what you need to know:

1) Multiple-choice Questions

Most popular of the short-answer questions is the "multiple choice" or "best answer" question. It can be used, for example, to test for factual knowledge, ability to solve problems or judgment in meeting situations found at work.

A multiple-choice question is normally one of three types—

- It can begin with an incomplete statement followed by several possible endings. You are to find the one ending which *best* completes the statement, although some of the others may not be entirely wrong.
- It can also be a complete statement in the form of a question which is answered by choosing one of the statements listed.
- It can be in the form of a problem – again you select the best answer.

Here is an example of a multiple-choice question with a discussion which should give you some clues as to the method for choosing the right answer:

When an employee has a complaint about his assignment, the action which will *best* help him overcome his difficulty is to
- A. discuss his difficulty with his coworkers
- B. take the problem to the head of the organization
- C. take the problem to the person who gave him the assignment
- D. say nothing to anyone about his complaint

In answering this question, you should study each of the choices to find which is best. Consider choice "A" – Certainly an employee may discuss his complaint with fellow employees, but no change or improvement can result, and the complaint remains unresolved. Choice "B" is a poor choice since the head of the organization probably does not know what assignment you have been given, and taking your problem to him is known as "going over the head" of the supervisor. The supervisor, or person who made the assignment, is the person who can clarify it or correct any injustice. Choice "C" is, therefore, correct. To say nothing, as in choice "D," is unwise. Supervisors have and interest in knowing the problems employees are facing, and the employee is seeking a solution to his problem.

2) True/False Questions

The "true/false" or "right/wrong" form of question is sometimes used. Here a complete statement is given. Your job is to decide whether the statement is right or wrong.

SAMPLE: A roaming cell-phone call to a nearby city costs less than a non-roaming call to a distant city.

This statement is wrong, or false, since roaming calls are more expensive.

This is not a complete list of all possible question forms, although most of the others are variations of these common types. You will always get complete directions for answering questions. Be sure you understand *how* to mark your answers – ask questions until you do.

V. RECORDING YOUR ANSWERS

Computer terminals are used more and more today for many different kinds of exams.

For an examination with very few applicants, you may be told to record your answers in the test booklet itself. Separate answer sheets are much more common. If this separate answer sheet is to be scored by machine – and this is often the case – it is highly important that you mark your answers correctly in order to get credit.

An electronic scoring machine is often used in civil service offices because of the speed with which papers can be scored. Machine-scored answer sheets must be marked with a pencil, which will be given to you. This pencil has a high graphite content which responds to the electronic scoring machine. As a matter of fact, stray dots may register as answers, so do not let your pencil rest on the answer sheet while you are pondering the correct answer. Also, if your pencil lead breaks or is otherwise defective, ask for another.

Since the answer sheet will be dropped in a slot in the scoring machine, be careful not to bend the corners or get the paper crumpled.

The answer sheet normally has five vertical columns of numbers, with 30 numbers to a column. These numbers correspond to the question numbers in your test booklet. After each number, going across the page are four or five pairs of dotted lines. These short dotted lines have small letters or numbers above them. The first two pairs may also have a "T" or "F" above the letters. This indicates that the first two pairs only are to be used if the questions are of the true-false type. If the questions are multiple choice, disregard the "T" and "F" and pay attention only to the small letters or numbers.

Answer your questions in the manner of the sample that follows:

32. The largest city in the United States is
    A. Washington, D.C.
    B. New York City
    C. Chicago
    D. Detroit
    E. San Francisco

1) Choose the answer you think is best. (New York City is the largest, so "B" is correct.)
2) Find the row of dotted lines numbered the same as the question you are answering. (Find row number 32)
3) Find the pair of dotted lines corresponding to the answer. (Find the pair of lines under the mark "B.")
4) Make a solid black mark between the dotted lines.

VI. BEFORE THE TEST

Common sense will help you find procedures to follow to get ready for an examination. Too many of us, however, overlook these sensible measures. Indeed, nervousness and fatigue have been found to be the most serious reasons why applicants fail to do their best on civil service tests. Here is a list of reminders:

- Begin your preparation early – Don't wait until the last minute to go scurrying around for books and materials or to find out what the position is all about.
- Prepare continuously – An hour a night for a week is better than an all-night cram session. This has been definitely established. What is more, a night a week for a month will return better dividends than crowding your study into a shorter period of time.
- Locate the place of the exam – You have been sent a notice telling you when and where to report for the examination. If the location is in a different town or otherwise unfamiliar to you, it would be well to inquire the best route and learn something about the building.
- Relax the night before the test – Allow your mind to rest. Do not study at all that night. Plan some mild recreation or diversion; then go to bed early and get a good night's sleep.
- Get up early enough to make a leisurely trip to the place for the test – This way unforeseen events, traffic snarls, unfamiliar buildings, etc. will not upset you.
- Dress comfortably – A written test is not a fashion show. You will be known by number and not by name, so wear something comfortable.
- Leave excess paraphernalia at home – Shopping bags and odd bundles will get in your way. You need bring only the items mentioned in the official notice you received; usually everything you need is provided. Do not bring reference books to the exam. They will only confuse those last minutes and be taken away from you when in the test room.
- Arrive somewhat ahead of time – If because of transportation schedules you must get there very early, bring a newspaper or magazine to take your mind off yourself while waiting.
- Locate the examination room – When you have found the proper room, you will be directed to the seat or part of the room where you will sit. Sometimes you are given a sheet of instructions to read while you are waiting. Do not fill out any forms until you are told to do so; just read them and be prepared.
- Relax and prepare to listen to the instructions
- If you have any physical problem that may keep you from doing your best, be sure to tell the test administrator. If you are sick or in poor health, you really cannot do your best on the exam. You can come back and take the test some other time.

VII. AT THE TEST

The day of the test is here and you have the test booklet in your hand. The temptation to get going is very strong. Caution! There is more to success than knowing the right answers. You must know how to identify your papers and understand variations in the type of short-answer question used in this particular examination. Follow these suggestions for maximum results from your efforts:

1) Cooperate with the monitor

The test administrator has a duty to create a situation in which you can be as much at ease as possible. He will give instructions, tell you when to begin, check to see that you are marking your answer sheet correctly, and so on. He is not there to guard you, although he will see that your competitors do not take unfair advantage. He wants to help you do your best.

2) Listen to all instructions

Don't jump the gun! Wait until you understand all directions. In most civil service tests you get more time than you need to answer the questions. So don't be in a hurry. Read each word of instructions until you clearly understand the meaning. Study the examples, listen to all announcements and follow directions. Ask questions if you do not understand what to do.

3) Identify your papers

Civil service exams are usually identified by number only. You will be assigned a number; you must not put your name on your test papers. Be sure to copy your number correctly. Since more than one exam may be given, copy your exact examination title.

4) Plan your time

Unless you are told that a test is a "speed" or "rate of work" test, speed itself is usually not important. Time enough to answer all the questions will be provided, but this does not mean that you have all day. An overall time limit has been set. Divide the total time (in minutes) by the number of questions to determine the approximate time you have for each question.

5) Do not linger over difficult questions

If you come across a difficult question, mark it with a paper clip (useful to have along) and come back to it when you have been through the booklet. One caution if you do this – be sure to skip a number on your answer sheet as well. Check often to be sure that you have not lost your place and that you are marking in the row numbered the same as the question you are answering.

6) Read the questions

Be sure you know what the question asks! Many capable people are unsuccessful because they failed to *read* the questions correctly.

7) Answer all questions

Unless you have been instructed that a penalty will be deducted for incorrect answers, it is better to guess than to omit a question.

8) Speed tests

It is often better NOT to guess on speed tests. It has been found that on timed tests people are tempted to spend the last few seconds before time is called in marking answers at random – without even reading them – in the hope of picking up a few extra points. To discourage this practice, the instructions may warn you that your score will be "corrected" for guessing. That is, a penalty will be applied. The incorrect answers will be deducted from the correct ones, or some other penalty formula will be used.

9) Review your answers

If you finish before time is called, go back to the questions you guessed or omitted to give them further thought. Review other answers if you have time.

10) Return your test materials

If you are ready to leave before others have finished or time is called, take ALL your materials to the monitor and leave quietly. Never take any test material with you. The monitor can discover whose papers are not complete, and taking a test booklet may be grounds for disqualification.

VIII. EXAMINATION TECHNIQUES

1) Read the general instructions carefully. These are usually printed on the first page of the exam booklet. As a rule, these instructions refer to the timing of the examination; the fact that you should not start work until the signal and must stop work at a signal, etc. If there are any *special* instructions, such as a choice of questions to be answered, make sure that you note this instruction carefully.

2) When you are ready to start work on the examination, that is as soon as the signal has been given, read the instructions to each question booklet, underline any key words or phrases, such as *least, best, outline, describe* and the like. In this way you will tend to answer as requested rather than discover on reviewing your paper that you *listed without describing*, that you selected the *worst* choice rather than the *best* choice, etc.

3) If the examination is of the objective or multiple-choice type – that is, each question will also give a series of possible answers: A, B, C or D, and you are called upon to select the best answer and write the letter next to that answer on your answer paper – it is advisable to start answering each question in turn. There may be anywhere from 50 to 100 such questions in the three or four hours allotted and you can see how much time would be taken if you read through all the questions before beginning to answer any. Furthermore, if you come across a question or group of questions which you know would be difficult to answer, it would undoubtedly affect your handling of all the other questions.

4) If the examination is of the essay type and contains but a few questions, it is a moot point as to whether you should read all the questions before starting to answer any one. Of course, if you are given a choice – say five out of seven and the like – then it is essential to read all the questions so you can eliminate the two that are most difficult. If, however, you are asked to answer all the questions, there may be danger in trying to answer the easiest one first because you may find that you will spend too much time on it. The best technique is to answer the first question, then proceed to the second, etc.

5) Time your answers. Before the exam begins, write down the time it started, then add the time allowed for the examination and write down the time it must be completed, then divide the time available somewhat as follows:

- If 3-1/2 hours are allowed, that would be 210 minutes. If you have 80 objective-type questions, that would be an average of 2-1/2 minutes per question. Allow yourself no more than 2 minutes per question, or a total of 160 minutes, which will permit about 50 minutes to review.
- If for the time allotment of 210 minutes there are 7 essay questions to answer, that would average about 30 minutes a question. Give yourself only 25 minutes per question so that you have about 35 minutes to review.

6) The most important instruction is to *read each question* and make sure you know what is wanted. The second most important instruction is to *time yourself properly* so that you answer every question. The third most important instruction is to *answer every question*. Guess if you have to but include something for each question. Remember that you will receive no credit for a blank and will probably receive some credit if you write something in answer to an essay question. If you guess a letter – say "B" for a multiple-choice question – you may have guessed right. If you leave a blank as an answer to a multiple-choice question, the examiners may respect your feelings but it will not add a point to your score. Some exams may penalize you for wrong answers, so in such cases *only*, you may not want to guess unless you have some basis for your answer.

7) Suggestions
   a. Objective-type questions
      1. Examine the question booklet for proper sequence of pages and questions
      2. Read all instructions carefully
      3. Skip any question which seems too difficult; return to it after all other questions have been answered
      4. Apportion your time properly; do not spend too much time on any single question or group of questions
      5. Note and underline key words – *all, most, fewest, least, best, worst, same, opposite,* etc.
      6. Pay particular attention to negatives
      7. Note unusual option, e.g., unduly long, short, complex, different or similar in content to the body of the question
      8. Observe the use of "hedging" words – *probably, may, most likely,* etc.
      9. Make sure that your answer is put next to the same number as the question
      10. Do not second-guess unless you have good reason to believe the second answer is definitely more correct
      11. Cross out original answer if you decide another answer is more accurate; do not erase until you are ready to hand your paper in
      12. Answer all questions; guess unless instructed otherwise
      13. Leave time for review

   b. Essay questions
      1. Read each question carefully
      2. Determine exactly what is wanted. Underline key words or phrases.
      3. Decide on outline or paragraph answer

4. Include many different points and elements unless asked to develop any one or two points or elements
5. Show impartiality by giving pros and cons unless directed to select one side only
6. Make and write down any assumptions you find necessary to answer the questions
7. Watch your English, grammar, punctuation and choice of words
8. Time your answers; don't crowd material

8) Answering the essay question

Most essay questions can be answered by framing the specific response around several key words or ideas. Here are a few such key words or ideas:

M's: manpower, materials, methods, money, management
P's: purpose, program, policy, plan, procedure, practice, problems, pitfalls, personnel, public relations
  a. Six basic steps in handling problems:
    1. Preliminary plan and background development
    2. Collect information, data and facts
    3. Analyze and interpret information, data and facts
    4. Analyze and develop solutions as well as make recommendations
    5. Prepare report and sell recommendations
    6. Install recommendations and follow up effectiveness

  b. Pitfalls to avoid
    1. *Taking things for granted* – A statement of the situation does not necessarily imply that each of the elements is necessarily true; for example, a complaint may be invalid and biased so that all that can be taken for granted is that a complaint has been registered
    2. *Considering only one side of a situation* – Wherever possible, indicate several alternatives and then point out the reasons you selected the best one
    3. *Failing to indicate follow up* – Whenever your answer indicates action on your part, make certain that you will take proper follow-up action to see how successful your recommendations, procedures or actions turn out to be
    4. *Taking too long in answering any single question* – Remember to time your answers properly

IX. AFTER THE TEST

Scoring procedures differ in detail among civil service jurisdictions although the general principles are the same. Whether the papers are hand-scored or graded by machine we have described, they are nearly always graded by number. That is, the person who marks the paper knows only the number – never the name – of the applicant. Not until all the papers have been graded will they be matched with names. If other tests, such as training and experience or oral interview ratings have been given, scores will be combined. Different parts of the examination usually have different weights. For example, the written test might count 60 percent of the final grade, and a rating of training and experience 40 percent. In many jurisdictions, veterans will have a certain number of points added to their grades.

After the final grade has been determined, the names are placed in grade order and an eligible list is established. There are various methods for resolving ties between those who get the same final grade – probably the most common is to place first the name of the person whose application was received first. Job offers are made from the eligible list in the order the names appear on it. You will be notified of your grade and your rank as soon as all these computations have been made. This will be done as rapidly as possible.

People who are found to meet the requirements in the announcement are called "eligibles." Their names are put on a list of eligible candidates. An eligible's chances of getting a job depend on how high he stands on this list and how fast agencies are filling jobs from the list.

When a job is to be filled from a list of eligibles, the agency asks for the names of people on the list of eligibles for that job. When the civil service commission receives this request, it sends to the agency the names of the three people highest on this list. Or, if the job to be filled has specialized requirements, the office sends the agency the names of the top three persons who meet these requirements from the general list.

The appointing officer makes a choice from among the three people whose names were sent to him. If the selected person accepts the appointment, the names of the others are put back on the list to be considered for future openings.

That is the rule in hiring from all kinds of eligible lists, whether they are for typist, carpenter, chemist, or something else. For every vacancy, the appointing officer has his choice of any one of the top three eligibles on the list. This explains why the person whose name is on top of the list sometimes does not get an appointment when some of the persons lower on the list do. If the appointing officer chooses the second or third eligible, the No. 1 eligible does not get a job at once, but stays on the list until he is appointed or the list is terminated.

X. HOW TO PASS THE INTERVIEW TEST

The examination for which you applied requires an oral interview test. You have already taken the written test and you are now being called for the interview test – the final part of the formal examination.

You may think that it is not possible to prepare for an interview test and that there are no procedures to follow during an interview. Our purpose is to point out some things you can do in advance that will help you and some good rules to follow and pitfalls to avoid while you are being interviewed.

What is an interview supposed to test?
The written examination is designed to test the technical knowledge and competence of the candidate; the oral is designed to evaluate intangible qualities, not readily measured otherwise, and to establish a list showing the relative fitness of each candidate – as measured against his competitors – for the position sought. Scoring is not on the basis of "right" and "wrong," but on a sliding scale of values ranging from "not passable" to "outstanding." As a matter of fact, it is possible to achieve a relatively low score without a single "incorrect" answer because of evident weakness in the qualities being measured.

Occasionally, an examination may consist entirely of an oral test – either an individual or a group oral. In such cases, information is sought concerning the technical knowledges and abilities of the candidate, since there has been no written examination for this purpose. More commonly, however, an oral test is used to supplement a written examination.

Who conducts interviews?

The composition of oral boards varies among different jurisdictions. In nearly all, a representative of the personnel department serves as chairman. One of the members of the board may be a representative of the department in which the candidate would work. In some cases, "outside experts" are used, and, frequently, a businessman or some other representative of the general public is asked to serve. Labor and management or other special groups may be represented. The aim is to secure the services of experts in the appropriate field.

However the board is composed, it is a good idea (and not at all improper or unethical) to ascertain in advance of the interview who the members are and what groups they represent. When you are introduced to them, you will have some idea of their backgrounds and interests, and at least you will not stutter and stammer over their names.

What should be done before the interview?

While knowledge about the board members is useful and takes some of the surprise element out of the interview, there is other preparation which is more substantive. It *is* possible to prepare for an oral interview – in several ways:

1) Keep a copy of your application and review it carefully before the interview

This may be the only document before the oral board, and the starting point of the interview. Know what education and experience you have listed there, and the sequence and dates of all of it. Sometimes the board will ask you to review the highlights of your experience for them; you should not have to hem and haw doing it.

2) Study the class specification and the examination announcement

Usually, the oral board has one or both of these to guide them. The qualities, characteristics or knowledges required by the position sought are stated in these documents. They offer valuable clues as to the nature of the oral interview. For example, if the job involves supervisory responsibilities, the announcement will usually indicate that knowledge of modern supervisory methods and the qualifications of the candidate as a supervisor will be tested. If so, you can expect such questions, frequently in the form of a hypothetical situation which you are expected to solve. NEVER go into an oral without knowledge of the duties and responsibilities of the job you seek.

3) Think through each qualification required

Try to visualize the kind of questions you would ask if you were a board member. How well could you answer them? Try especially to appraise your own knowledge and background in each area, *measured against the job sought*, and identify any areas in which you are weak. Be critical and realistic – do not flatter yourself.

4) Do some general reading in areas in which you feel you may be weak

For example, if the job involves supervision and your past experience has NOT, some general reading in supervisory methods and practices, particularly in the field of human relations, might be useful. Do NOT study agency procedures or detailed manuals. The oral board will be testing your understanding and capacity, not your memory.

5) Get a good night's sleep and watch your general health and mental attitude

You will want a clear head at the interview. Take care of a cold or any other minor ailment, and of course, no hangovers.

What should be done on the day of the interview?

Now comes the day of the interview itself. Give yourself plenty of time to get there. Plan to arrive somewhat ahead of the scheduled time, particularly if your appointment is in the fore part of the day. If a previous candidate fails to appear, the board might be ready for you a bit early. By early afternoon an oral board is almost invariably behind schedule if there are many candidates, and you may have to wait. Take along a book or magazine to read, or your application to review, but leave any extraneous material in the waiting room when you go in for your interview. In any event, relax and compose yourself.

The matter of dress is important. The board is forming impressions about you – from your experience, your manners, your attitude, and your appearance. Give your personal appearance careful attention. Dress your best, but not your flashiest. Choose conservative, appropriate clothing, and be sure it is immaculate. This is a business interview, and your appearance should indicate that you regard it as such. Besides, being well groomed and properly dressed will help boost your confidence.

Sooner or later, someone will call your name and escort you into the interview room. *This is it.* From here on you are on your own. It is too late for any more preparation. But remember, you asked for this opportunity to prove your fitness, and you are here because your request was granted.

What happens when you go in?

The usual sequence of events will be as follows: The clerk (who is often the board stenographer) will introduce you to the chairman of the oral board, who will introduce you to the other members of the board. Acknowledge the introductions before you sit down. Do not be surprised if you find a microphone facing you or a stenotypist sitting by. Oral interviews are usually recorded in the event of an appeal or other review.

Usually the chairman of the board will open the interview by reviewing the highlights of your education and work experience from your application – primarily for the benefit of the other members of the board, as well as to get the material into the record. Do not interrupt or comment unless there is an error or significant misinterpretation; if that is the case, do not hesitate. But do not quibble about insignificant matters. Also, he will usually ask you some question about your education, experience or your present job – partly to get you to start talking and to establish the interviewing "rapport." He may start the actual questioning, or turn it over to one of the other members. Frequently, each member undertakes the questioning on a particular area, one in which he is perhaps most competent, so you can expect each member to participate in the examination. Because time is limited, you may also expect some rather abrupt switches in the direction the questioning takes, so do not be upset by it. Normally, a board member will not pursue a single line of questioning unless he discovers a particular strength or weakness.

After each member has participated, the chairman will usually ask whether any member has any further questions, then will ask you if you have anything you wish to add. Unless you are expecting this question, it may floor you. Worse, it may start you off on an extended, extemporaneous speech. The board is not usually seeking more information. The question is principally to offer you a last opportunity to present further qualifications or to indicate that you have nothing to add. So, if you feel that a significant qualification or characteristic has been overlooked, it is proper to point it out in a sentence or so. Do not compliment the board on the thoroughness of their examination – they have been sketchy, and you know it. If you wish, merely say, "No thank you, I have nothing further to add." This is a point where you can "talk yourself out" of a good impression or fail to present an important bit of information. Remember, *you close the interview yourself.*

The chairman will then say, "That is all, Mr. _____, thank you." Do not be startled; the interview is over, and quicker than you think. Thank him, gather your belongings and take your leave. Save your sigh of relief for the other side of the door.

How to put your best foot forward

Throughout this entire process, you may feel that the board individually and collectively is trying to pierce your defenses, seek out your hidden weaknesses and embarrass and confuse you. Actually, this is not true. They are obliged to make an appraisal of your qualifications for the job you are seeking, and they want to see you in your best light. Remember, they must interview all candidates and a non-cooperative candidate may become a failure in spite of their best efforts to bring out his qualifications. Here are 15 suggestions that will help you:

1) Be natural – Keep your attitude confident, not cocky

If you are not confident that you can do the job, do not expect the board to be. Do not apologize for your weaknesses, try to bring out your strong points. The board is interested in a positive, not negative, presentation. Cockiness will antagonize any board member and make him wonder if you are covering up a weakness by a false show of strength.

2) Get comfortable, but don't lounge or sprawl

Sit erectly but not stiffly. A careless posture may lead the board to conclude that you are careless in other things, or at least that you are not impressed by the importance of the occasion. Either conclusion is natural, even if incorrect. Do not fuss with your clothing, a pencil or an ashtray. Your hands may occasionally be useful to emphasize a point; do not let them become a point of distraction.

3) Do not wisecrack or make small talk

This is a serious situation, and your attitude should show that you consider it as such. Further, the time of the board is limited – they do not want to waste it, and neither should you.

4) Do not exaggerate your experience or abilities

In the first place, from information in the application or other interviews and sources, the board may know more about you than you think. Secondly, you probably will not get away with it. An experienced board is rather adept at spotting such a situation, so do not take the chance.

5) If you know a board member, do not make a point of it, yet do not hide it

Certainly you are not fooling him, and probably not the other members of the board. Do not try to take advantage of your acquaintanceship – it will probably do you little good.

6) Do not dominate the interview

Let the board do that. They will give you the clues – do not assume that you have to do all the talking. Realize that the board has a number of questions to ask you, and do not try to take up all the interview time by showing off your extensive knowledge of the answer to the first one.

7) Be attentive

You only have 20 minutes or so, and you should keep your attention at its sharpest throughout. When a member is addressing a problem or question to you, give him your undivided attention. Address your reply principally to him, but do not exclude the other board members.

8) Do not interrupt

A board member may be stating a problem for you to analyze. He will ask you a question when the time comes. Let him state the problem, and wait for the question.

9) Make sure you understand the question

Do not try to answer until you are sure what the question is. If it is not clear, restate it in your own words or ask the board member to clarify it for you. However, do not haggle about minor elements.

10) Reply promptly but not hastily

A common entry on oral board rating sheets is "candidate responded readily," or "candidate hesitated in replies." Respond as promptly and quickly as you can, but do not jump to a hasty, ill-considered answer.

11) Do not be peremptory in your answers

A brief answer is proper – but do not fire your answer back. That is a losing game from your point of view. The board member can probably ask questions much faster than you can answer them.

12) Do not try to create the answer you think the board member wants

He is interested in what kind of mind you have and how it works – not in playing games. Furthermore, he can usually spot this practice and will actually grade you down on it.

13) Do not switch sides in your reply merely to agree with a board member

Frequently, a member will take a contrary position merely to draw you out and to see if you are willing and able to defend your point of view. Do not start a debate, yet do not surrender a good position. If a position is worth taking, it is worth defending.

14) Do not be afraid to admit an error in judgment if you are shown to be wrong

The board knows that you are forced to reply without any opportunity for careful consideration. Your answer may be demonstrably wrong. If so, admit it and get on with the interview.

15) Do not dwell at length on your present job

The opening question may relate to your present assignment. Answer the question but do not go into an extended discussion. You are being examined for a *new* job, not your present one. As a matter of fact, try to phrase ALL your answers in terms of the job for which you are being examined.

Basis of Rating

Probably you will forget most of these "do's" and "don'ts" when you walk into the oral interview room. Even remembering them all will not ensure you a passing grade. Perhaps you did not have the qualifications in the first place. But remembering them will help you to put your best foot forward, without treading on the toes of the board members.

Rumor and popular opinion to the contrary notwithstanding, an oral board wants you to make the best appearance possible. They know you are under pressure – but they also want to see how you respond to it as a guide to what your reaction would be under the pressures of the job you seek. They will be influenced by the degree of poise you display, the personal traits you show and the manner in which you respond.

ABOUT THIS BOOK

This book contains tests divided into Examination Sections. Go through each test, answering every question in the margin. At the end of each test look at the answer key and check your answers. On the ones you got wrong, look at the right answer choice and learn. Do not fill in the answers first. Do not memorize the questions and answers, but understand the answer and principles involved. On your test, the questions will likely be different from the samples. Questions are changed and new ones added. If you understand these past questions you should have success with any changes that arise. Tests may consist of several types of questions. We have additional books on each subject should more study be advisable or necessary for you. Finally, the more you study, the better prepared you will be. This book is intended to be the last thing you study before you walk into the examination room. Prior study of relevant texts is also recommended. NLC publishes some of these in our Fundamental Series. Knowledge and good sense are important factors in passing your exam. Good luck also helps. So now study this Passbook, absorb the material contained within and take that knowledge into the examination. Then do your best to pass that exam.

EXAMINATION SECTION

EXAMINATION SECTION
TEST 1

DIRECTIONS: Each question or incomplete statement is followed by several suggested answers or completions. Select the one that *BEST* answers the question or completes the statement. *PRINT THE LETTER OF THE CORRECT ANSWER IN THE SPACE AT THE RIGHT.*

1. When a security officer fails to report to work in time to make his scheduled relief, the security officer on duty must call the foreman immediately.
The *MAIN* reason for this procedure is to

    A. make sure that the security officer on duty is not overworked
    B. make a record of the number of times that a security officer is late
    C. make sure that Authority property and materials are continuously guarded
    D. prevent the security officer who is late from being paid for the time that he did not work

1.____

2. A security officer must report to his foreman any employee who is on Authority property in an intoxicated condition.
The *MAIN* reason for this procedure is that

    A. this employee may give the general public the impression that many Authority employees drink while on duty
    B. an employee who drinks on the job may encourage fellow employees to also drink on the job
    C. an intoxicated employee may endanger himself and other Authority employees
    D. the intoxicated employee's foreman may not have noticed this condition

2.____

3. If a security officer is required to make hourly calls to his foreman within twenty minutes of the hour, a correct time for a security officer to make his hourly call is at

    A. 3:36 A.M.   B. 8:29 A.M.   C. 4:27 A.M.   D. 7:48 P.M.

3.____

4. Which of the following characteristics of a security officer doing record keeping is *MOST* important?

    A. Familiarity with rules and procedures
    B. An analytical mind
    C. Accuracy
    D. Speed

4.____

5. Of the following, the type of equipment that a security officer working a 12:00 midnight to 8:00 A.M. shift would be expected to use *MOST* often is a

    A. pistol   B. flashlight   C. camera   D. siren

5.____

6. Before going on duty, a security officer is required to read all new bulletins posted on the bulletin board. The *MAIN* reason for this requirement is to

    A. acquaint the security officer with new regulations
    B. make sure that the security officer understands all the rules
    C. make the security officer responsible for any violations of the rules
    D. acquaint the security officer with his rights

6.____

7. Assume that soon after being appointed as a security officer, you decide that some of the rules and regulations of the Authority are unwise.
Of the following, you should

    A. disregard these rules and regulations and use your own good judgment
    B. not do your job until some changes are made
    C. make the changes that you decide are necessary
    D. carry out these rules and regulations regardless of your opinion

7.____

Questions 8-11.
DIRECTIONS: Questions 8 to 11 are based on information contained in LOCATION OF KEY STATIONS shown below. When answering these questions, refer to this information.

LOCATION OF KEY STATIONS

No. 12 key station - located on double fire exit door adjacent to Briarcliff Avenue vehicle ramp.
No. 13 key station - located on wall adjacent to fire exit door in Unit Repair Section.
No. 14 key station - located in men's locker room on door leading to washroom near water cooler.
No. 15 key station - located in corridor leading to transportation area on wall adjacent to room number 1 and opposite to first aid room.
No. 16 key station - located on wall adjacent to door leading into unit storeroom.
No. 17 key station - located on a wall adjacent to double fire exit doors in Unit Repair Section.
No. 18 key station - located on wall adjacent to fire exit door in body shop.

8. Two key stations are located on or near double fire exit doors. One of them is key station No. 12.
The *other* is key station No.

    A. 13   B. 14   C. 17   D. 18

8.____

9. If a security officer took a drink of water, he would *MOST* likely do so at a location closest to key station No.

    A. 12   B. 14   C. 16   D. 17

9.____

10. A delivery of $759.00 worth of supplies would *MOST* likely be made to a location which is closest to key station No.

    A. 13   B. 14   C. 16   D. 18

10.____

11. A fire exit door will *NOT* be found at key station No.

    A. 12   B. 13   C. 15   D. 17

11.____

12. When preparing a report, a security officer should generally make *at least* one extra copy so that

    A. it can be sent to a newspaper
    B. there will be no mistakes made
    C. a personal record can be kept
    D. the information in the report can be discussed by all other security officers

12.____

13. In writing a report about a storeroom robbery by several men, the *LEAST* important of the following information is   13.____

     A. the number of men involved
     B. a list of the items that were stolen
     C. how the men entered the storeroom
     D. how many lights were left on by the robbers

Questions 14-19.

DIRECTIONS: Questions 14 to 19 are based on the paragraph REGISTRY SHEETS shown below. When answering these questions, refer to this paragraph.

REGISTRY SHEETS

Where registry sheets are in effect, the security officer must legibly print Authority employee's pass number, title, license and vehicle number, destination, time in and time out; and each Authority employee must sign his or her name. The same procedure is to be applied to visitors, except in place of a pass number each visitor will indicate his address or firm name; and visitors must also sign waivers. Information is to be obtained from driver's license, firm credential card, or any other appropriate identification, All visitors must state their purpose for entering upon the property. If they desire to visit anyone, verification must be made before entry is permitted. All persons signing sheet must sign in when entering upon the property, and sign out again when leaving. The security officer will, at the end of his tour, draw a horizontal line across the entire sheet after his last entry, indicating the end of one tour and the beginning of another. At the top of each sheet the security officer will enter the number of entries made during his tour, the sheet number, post, and date. Sheets are to begin with number 1 on the first day of the month, and should be kept in numerical order. Each security officer will read the orders at each post to see whether any changes are made and at which hours control sheets are in effect.

14. Waivers need *NOT* be signed by   14.____

     A. Authority employees   B. vendors
     C. reporters   D. salesmen

15. All visitors are required to state   15.____

     A. whether they have a criminal record
     B. the reason for their visit
     C. the reason they are not bonded
     D. whether they have ever worked for the Authority

16. In the paragraph, the statement is made that "verification must be made before entry is permitted." The word *verification* means, most nearly,   16.____

     A. allowance   B. confirmation   C. refusal   D. disposal

17. A security officer must draw a horizontal line across the entire registry sheet in order to show that   17.____

     A. he is being replaced to check a disturbance outside
     B. the last tour for the day has been completed
     C. one tour is ending and another is beginning
     D. a visitor has finished his business and is leaving

18. At the top of a registry sheet, it is *NOT* necessary for a security officer to list the   18.____

    A. tour number   B. number of entries made
    C. sheet number   D. date

19. A security officer should check at which hours control sheets are in effect by reading   19.____

    A. registry sheet number 1, on the first day of each month
    B. the orders at each post
    C. the time in and time out that each person has entered on the registry sheet
    D. the last entry made on the registry sheet used before the start of his tour

20. Assume that after working as a security officer for some time, your foreman is replaced   20.____
by a new foreman.
If this new foreman insists on explaining to you the procedure for doing a job which you
know how to do very well, you should listen to the new foreman *MAINLY* because

    A. you may catch him in an error and thus prove you know your job
    B. it is wise to humor a foreman even when he is wrong
    C. you can do the job the way you like after the foreman leaves
    D. it will be your responsibility to perform the job the way the new foreman wants it
       done

21. All security officers are instructed that whenever they report an accident to the main   21.____
office by telephone, prior to preparing their written accident report, they should request
the name of the person receiving the call and also make a note of the time.
The *MAIN* purpose of this precaution is to fix responsibility for the

    A. cause of the accident
    B. recording of the accident at the main office
    C. accuracy of the accident report
    D. preparation of the written report

22. One of your duties as a security officer will be to compile the facts about an accident in a   22.____
written report. The *LEAST* important item to include in such an accident report is

    A. the people involved
    B. what action you took
    C. the extent of personal injuries
    D. why you think the accident happened

23. It is *MOST* important for a written report to be   23.____

    A. accurate   B. brief
    C. detailed   D. properly punctuated

24. In a large bus shop where many security officers are used, each security officer is   24.____
required to do his work in a definite prescribed manner *MAINLY* because

    A. this practice insures discipline
    B. no other method will work
    C. this practice will keep the security officer from being inattentive on the job
    D. there will be less need for the security officers to consult with their supervisors

25. When an unusual situation arises on the job, and it would take too long for you to contact   25._____
your foreman for advice, the *BEST* procedure for you to follow is to

    A.   play it safe and take no action
    B.   confer with another security officer
    C.   check your rule book for the proper procedure
    D.   act according to your best judgment

26. At the scene of an accident it is good first-aid procedure to treat the most badly injured   26._____
person first. Of the following injured people, the person *LEAST* in need of immediate care
is one who

    A.   is bleeding rapidly
    B.   finds great difficulty in breathing
    C.   appears to have sprained an ankle
    D.   complains of severe pains in his chest

Questions 27-32.

DIRECTIONS: Questions 27 to 32 are based on the paragraph THEFT shown below. When
answering these questions, refer to this paragraph.

THEFT

    A security officer must be alert at all times to discourage the willful removal of property
and material of the Authority by individuals for self gain. Should a security officer detect such
an individual, he should detain him and immediately call the supervisor at that location. No
force should be used during the process of detainment. However, should the individual bolt
from the premises, the security officer will be expected to offer some clues for his apprehension. Therefore, he should try to remember some characteristic traits about the individual,
such as clothing, height, coloring, speech, and how he made his approach. Unusual characteristics such as a scar or a limp are most important. If a car is used, the security officer
should take the license plate number of said car. Above information should be supplied to the
responding peace officer and the special inspection control desk. In desolate locations, the
security officer should first call the police and then the special inspection control desk. Any
security officer having information of the theft should contact the director of special inspection
by telephone or by mail. This information will be kept confidential if desired.

27. A security officer is required to be attentive on the job at all times, *MAINLY* to   27._____

    A.   get as much work done as possible
    B.   prevent the stealing of Authority property
    C.   show his supervisor that he is doing a good job
    D.   prevent any other security officer from patrolling the area to which he is assigned

28. In the second sentence, the word *detain* means, most nearly,   28._____

    A.   delay   B.   avoid   C.   call   D.   report

29. The prescribed course of action a security officer should take when he discovers a per-   29._____
son stealing Authority property is to

    A.   make sure that all gates are closed to prevent the thief from escaping
    B.   detain the thief and quickly call the supervisor

C. use his club to keep the thief there until the police arrive
D. call another security officer for assistance

30. The *MOST* useful of the following descriptions of a runaway thief would be that he is a   30.____

    A. tall man who runs fast   B. man with blue eyes
    C. man with black hair   D. tall man who limps

31. The license plate number of a car which is used by a thief to escape should be reported   31.____
by & security officer to the responding peace officer *and* the

    A. director of protection agents
    B. security officer's supervisor
    C. special inspection control desk
    D. department of motor vehicles

32. A security officer patrolling a desolate area has spotted a thief. The security officer   32.____
should *FIRST* call

    A. his supervisor
    B. the police
    C. the special inspection control desk
    D. the director of special inspection

33. It is very important that Authority officials be given legible hand-written reports on   33.____
unusual occurrences if there is no time to type them up.
According to the above statement about hand-written reports, it would be *MOST* useful
if a security officer, when writing a report,

    A. did not write on the back of the page
    B. did not use big words
    C. wrote concisely
    D. wrote out all the information clearly

34. A security officer sees a youth marking up the wall surrounding Authority property. He   34.____
should *FIRST*

    A. tell the youth to stop   B. arrest the youth
    C. call a policeman   D. punish the youth

35. If an alarm goes off and a security officer observes a van speeding away from a store-   35.____
room, the information that would be *LEAST* helpful in identifying the van would be the

    A. color of the van
    B. approximate speed at which the van passed his post
    C. state and the license plate number of the van
    D. manufacturer and model of the van

36. A security officer notices that a power line, knocked down by a storm, has electrified a   36.____
steel flagpole. After notifying his supervisor, of the following it would be *BEST* to

    A. put a wooden "caution" sign on the flagpole and call the Fire Department
    B. remove the wire from the flagpole
    C. stay near the flagpole and warn everyone not to go near the flagpole
    D. say nothing about it until his supervisor arrives

37. Another Authority employee informs a security officer, who is on duty at the entrance to an Authority bus depot, that he has found a bomb in the locker room. The security officer should *FIRST*

    A. investigate to see if it is actually a bomb
    B. clear the area of persons in or near the locker room
    C. question the man closely to determine if he really saw a bomb
    D. call the Bomb Squad for instructions on handling bombs

37.____

38. In *MOST* cases, a written report on an accident is *better* than an oral report because a written report

    A. can be referred to later
    B. takes less time to prepare
    C. includes more of the facts
    D. reduces the number of court cases

38.____

39. A report of an accident is *MOST* likely to be accurate if written by the security officer

    A. long after the event
    B. after taking about a week to make sure he has all the facts
    C. immediately after the event
    D. after thoroughly discussing the event with others for several days

39.____

40. The gross weight of a carton and its contents is 830.2 pounds. If the weight of the carton alone is 98.7 pounds, the net weight of the contents of the carton is

    A. 731.5 pounds   B. 732.5 pounds
    C. 741.5 pounds   D. 831.5 pounds

40.____

KEY (CORRECT ANSWERS)

1.	C	11.	C	21.	B	31.	C
2.	C	12.	C	22.	D	32.	B
3.	D	13.	D	23.	A	33.	D
4.	C	14.	A	24.	D	34.	A
5.	B	15.	B	25.	D	35.	B
6.	A	16.	B	26.	C	36.	C
7.	D	17.	C	27.	B	37.	B
8.	C	18.	A	28.	A	38.	A
9.	B	19.	B	29.	B	39.	C
10.	C	20.	D	30.	D	40.	A

TEST 2

DIRECTIONS: Each question or incomplete statement is followed by several suggested answers or completions. Select the one that *BEST* answers the question or completes the statement. *PRINT THE LETTER OF THE CORRECT ANSWER TN THE SPACE AT THE RIGHT.*

Questions 1-10.

DIRECTIONS: Read the DESCRIPTION OF ACCIDENT carefully. Then answer Questions 1 to 10, inclusive, using only this information in picking your answer.

DESCRIPTION OF ACCIDENT

On Friday, May 9th, at about 2:30 p.m, Bus Operator Joe Able, badge no, 1234, was operating his half-filled bus, Authority no. 5678, northbound along Fifth Ave., when a green Ford truck, N.Y. license no. 9012, driven by Sam Wood, came out of an Authority storeroom entrance into the path of the bus. To avoid hitting the truck, Joe Able turned his steering wheel sharply to the left, causing his bus to cross the solid white line into the opposite lane where the bus crashed head-on into a black 1975 Mercury, N.Y. license no. 3456, driven by Bill Green. The crash caused the Mercury to sideswipe a blue VW, N.J. license 7890, driven by Jim White, which was double-parked while he made a delivery. The sudden movement of the bus caused one of the passengers, Mrs. Jane Smith, to fall, striking her head on one of the seats, Joe Able blew his horn vigorously to summon aid and Security Officer Fred Norton, badge no. 9876, and Stockman Al Blue, badge no. 5432, came out of the storeroom and rendered assistance. While Norton gave Mrs. Smith first aid, Blue summoned an ambulance for Green. A tow truck removed Green's car and Able found that the bus could operate under its own power, so he returned to the garage.

1. The Ford truck was driven by   1._____

    A. Able   B. Green   C. Wood   D. White

2. The Authority no. of the bus was   2._____

    A. 1234   B. 5678   C. 9012   D. 3456

3. The bus was driven by   3._____

    A. Able   B. Green   C. Wood   D. White

4. The license no. of the VW was   4._____

    A. 9012   B. 3456   C. 7890   D. 5432

5. The horn of the bus summoned   5._____

    A. Blue   B. Green   C. White   D. Smith

6. The badge no. of the security officer was   6._____

    A. 5432   B. 5678   C. 1234   D. 9876

7. The Mercury was driven by   7._____

    A. Smith   B. Norton   C. White   D. Green

8. The bus was traveling   8.____

    A. North   B. East   C. South   D. West

9. The vehicle towed away was a   9.____

    A. bus   B. Ford   C. Mercury   D. VW

10. Mrs. Smith hurt her   10.____

    A. head   B. back   C. arm   D. leg

11. If more than one security officer is involved in an incident, each is required to write a   11.____
report giving his version of what happened. By having *both* reports submitted, the information gathered

    A. should be more complete
    B. should clear the Authority from any blame
    C. cannot be disputed
    D. will not be opinionated

12. If a security officer gets $5.42 per hour, and $8.13 per hour for overtime work, his *gross*   12.____
salary for a week in which he works 5 hours over his regular 40 hours is

    A. $216.80   B. $243.90   C. $257.45   D. $325.20

13. It takes 2 min. 45 sec. for a security officer to travel to his first clock station, 3 min. to get   13.____
to the second, 2 min. to get to the third, 5 1/2 min. to get to the fourth, and 4 min. 15 sec.
to get from the fourth back to the starting point.
Neglecting the time spent at each clock station, the *TOTAL* time needed to make one
round tour is

    A. 16 min. 45 sec.   B. 17 min. 15 sec.
    C. 17 min. 30 sec.   D. 18 min.

Questions 14-20.

DIRECTIONS: Questions 14 to 20 are based on the rules listed below and are numbered 1 to
7. Each question gives a situation in which a security officer has disobeyed at
least one rule. For each question, select from among the four choices the
number of a rule which the security officer has disobeyed.

Rule Number 1:   A security officer is subject to the orders of foremen (security officer) and of
employees assigned to the special inspection control desk.

Rule Number 2:   A security officer must protect system properties against fire, theft, vandalism,
and unauthorized entrance.

Rule Number 3:   A security officer is responsible for all equipment and other property entrusted
to him and must see that such equipment is kept in good condition.

Rule Number 4:   A security officer must give information about an accident only to authorized
Authority officials.

Rule Number 5: A security officer must be attired in the prescribed uniform with badge displayed at all times while on duty.

Rule Number 6: A security officer must remain on duty during his entire tour and must therefore eat lunch on the job.

Rule Number 7: A security officer must not allow another employee to perform any part of his
duties without proper authority.

14. While investigating a noise in the parking lot at night, Security Officer Johnson could not   14.____
see very well because his flashlight was not in working order. Johnson disobeyed Rule
Number

    A. 1   B. 3   C. 5   D. 7

15. Without getting permission to do so, Security Officer Simpson went to the locker room to   15.____
get his lunch and let the porter, Baxter, check the credentials of a truck driver whose
truck was about to enter Authority property. Simpson disobeyed Rule Number

    A. 1   B. 3   C. 5   D. 7

16. After being told by his foreman to check the door of Storeroom No. 15 before leaving,   16.____
Security Officer Roscoe went off duty before seeing whether or not the door was properly
locked. Roscoe disobeyed Rule Number

    A. 1   B. 4   C. 6   D. 7

17. Security Officer Andrews removed his badge ten minutes before going off duty. Andrews   17.____
disobeyed Rule Number

    A. 2   B. 4   C. 5   D. 6

18. Security Officer Paul left his post inside the train yard in order to make a personal tele-   18.____
phone call. As a result, Paul disobeyed Rule Number

    A. 2   B. 4   C. 5   D. 7

19. Security Officer Burroughs gave a newspaper reporter details of an accident that   19.____
occurred on his post. Burroughs disobeyed Rule Number

    A. 1   B. 2   C. 3   D. 4

20. Security Officer Grenich left his post unattended and went across the street to a diner,   20.____
since he left his lunch at home. Grenich disobeyed Rule Number

    A. 4   B. 5   C. 6   D. 7

Questions 21-25.

DIRECTIONS: Questions 21 to 25 are based on the UNUSUAL OCCURRENCE REPORT
given below. Five phrases in the report have been removed and are listed
below the report as 1. through 5. In each of the five places where phrases of
the report have been left out, the number of a question has been inserted. For
each question, select the number of the missing phrase which would make the
report read correctly.

UNUSUAL OCCURRENCE REPORT

Post 20A
Tour 12 a.m.-8 a.m.
Date August 13

Location of Occurrence: Storeroom #55

REMARKS: While making rounds this morning I thought that I heard some strange sounds coming from Storeroom #55. Upon investigation, I saw that 21 and that the door to the storeroom was slightly opened. At 2:45 a.m. I 22 .

Suddenly two men jumped out from 23 , dropped the tools which they were holding, and made a dash for the door. I ordered them to stop, but they just kept running.

I was able to get a good look at both of them. One man was wearing a green jacket and had a full beard and the other was short and had blond hair. Immediately, I called the police and about two minutes later I notified 24 . I 25 the police arrived and I gave them the complete details of the incident.

Security Officer Donald Rimson 23807
Signature Pass No.

1.   the special inspection control desk
2.   behind some crates
3.   the lock had been tampered with
4.   remained at the storeroom until
5.   entered the storeroom and began to look around

21.   A. 1   B. 3   C. 4   D. 5   21.____

22.   A. 2   B. 3   C. 4   D. 5   22.____

23.   A. 1   B. 2   C. 3   D. 4   23.____

24.   A. 1   B. 2   C. 3   D. 4   24.____

25.   A. 2   B. 3   C. 4   D. 5   25.____

26.   Employees using supplies from a first-aid kit are generally required to submit an immediate report on what happened and what supplies were used.
Of the following, the *MOST* important reason for this regulation is to   26.____

   A.   make sure that supplies which are used are replaced
   B.   prevent theft
   C.   see that the correct employee gets credit for taking action
   D.   identify the person who last used the kit

27.   The log book of a security officer stationed at an entry gate shows 47 entries in two hours. At this rate, the number of entries in eight hours is   27.____

   A.   108   B.   168   C.   188   D.   376

28.   A truck driver leaving Authority property has a requisition form showing 14 cartons of pencils, 12 cartons of pens, 27 cartons of envelopes, and 39 cartons of writing pads. If an actual count of the cartons on the truck shows only 77 cartons, the number of cartons missing is   28.____

   A.   15   B.   14   C.   12   D.   5

29. It is *NOT* advisable to move an injured man before the arrival of a doctor if the man has   29.____

    A. a severe nosebleed
                    B. burns over 3% of his body
    C. fainted from the heat
                    D. possibly injured his spine

30. While making rounds during daylight hours, a security officer notices that one of the   30.____
floodlights in the parking lot has been left on. The security officer should

    A. turn the light off because it will cost him his job if his foreman finds out about this
    B. turn the light off, because it is not needed
    C. leave the light on and call his foreman to investigate
    D. leave the light on to make it easier for him to see anything which looks suspicious

31. A security officer comes upon an empty fire extinguisher while making his rounds. Of the   31.____
following, it is *MOST* important that he

    A. ignore it, since mentioning this might get someone into trouble
    B. make a note not to use that extinguisher in case of a fire
    C. report it to the next security officer who relieves him
    D. report it to his foreman

32. The windows of the booth used by a security officer must be kept clean and clear of any   32.____
obstructions at all times. The *MOST* obvious reason for this is to

    A. enable anyone passing by the booth to look into it and see who is on duty
    B. allow as much daylight as possible to enter the booth so that a security officer can
conserve electricity by keeping booth lights turned off
    C. enable a security officer to see what is happening outside of the booth
    D. make certain that a security officer makes a good impression on inspectors who
are passing by the booth

33. A security officer must be completely familiar with door schedules (when the door must   33.____
be locked and when open), particularly during hours when employees are reporting for
work.
If a security officer does not know all door schedules for his post it would be *BEST* for
him to

    A. quickly get a copy of the door schedule from the security officer who will relieve him
    B. check the bulletin board at a nearby post to see if he can get a copy of the door
schedules
    C. let his foreman know about it immediately, so the foreman can give him the infor-
mation he needs
    D. check the rules and regulations book for the information

Questions 34-37.

DIRECTIONS: Questions 34 to 37 inclusive are based on the paragraph FIRE FIGHTING
                   shown below. When answering these questions, refer to this paragraph.

FIRE FIGHTING

A security officer should remember the cardinal rule that water or soda acid fire extinguishers should not be used on any electrical fire, and apply it in the case of a fire near the third rail. In addition, security officers should familiarize themselves with all available fire alarms and fire-fighting equipment within their assigned posts. Use of the fire alarm should bring responding Fire Department apparatus quickly to the scene. Familiarity with the fire-fighting equipment near his post would help in putting out incipient fires. Any man calling for the Fire Department should remain outside so that he can direct the Fire Department to the fire. As soon as possible thereafter, the special inspection desk must be notified and a complete written report of the fire, no matter how small, must be submitted to this office. The security officer must give the exact time and place it started, who discovered it, how it was extinguished, the damage done, cause of same, list of any injured persons with the extent of their injuries, and the name of the Fire Chief in charge. All defects noticed by the security officer concerning the fire alarm or any firefighting equipment must be reported to the special inspection department.

34. It would be proper to use water to put out a fire in a(n)   34.____

    A. electric motor   B. electric switch box
    C. waste paper trash can   D. electric generator

35. After calling the Fire Department from a street box to report a fire, the security officer   35.____
    should then

    A. return to the fire and help put it out
    B. stay outside and direct the Fire Department to the fire
    C. find a phone and call his boss
    D. write out a report for the special inspection desk

36. A security officer is required to submit a complete written report of a fire   36.____

    A. two weeks after the fire
    B. the day following the fire
    C. as soon as possible
    D.   at his convenience

37. In his report of a fire, it is *NOT* necessary for the security officer to state   37.____

    A. time and place of the fire
    B. who discovered the fire
    C. the names of persons injured
    D. quantity of Fire Department equipment used

38. While making afternoon rounds, a security officer climbs a stairway which has a loose   38.____
    banister.
    To avoid having someone injured, the security officer should

    A. inform his foreman of the hazard so that it can be corrected
    B. fix the banister himself, since it can probably be fixed quickly
    C. block the stairway with rope at the top and bottom so that no one else can use it
    D. put up a caution sign in the hallway leading to the stairway

39. If, while on duty, a security officer sees an accident which results in injuries to Authority employees, it would be most important for him to *FIRST*

    39.____

    A. render all possible first-aid to the injured
    B. record the exact time the accident happened
    C. write out an accident report
    D. try to find out what caused the accident

40. If a security officer has many accidents, no matter what shift or location he is assigned to, the *MOST* likely reason for this is

    40.____

    A. lack of safety devices
    B. not enough safety posters
    C. inferior equipment and materials
    D. careless work practices

KEY (CORRECT ANSWERS)

1.	C	11.	A	21.	B	31.	D
2.	B	12.	C	22.	D	32.	C
3.	A	13.	C	23.	B	33.	C
4.	C	14.	B	24.	A	34.	C
5.	A	15.	D	25.	C	35.	B
6.	D	16.	A	26.	A	36.	C
7.	D	17.	C	27.	C	37.	D
8.	A	18.	A	28.	A	38.	A
9.	C	19.	D	29.	D	39.	A
10.	A	20.	C	30.	B	40.	D

EXAMINATION SECTION
TEST 1

DIRECTIONS: Each question or incomplete statement is followed by several suggested answers or completions. Select the one that BEST answers the question or completes the statement. *PRINT THE LETTER OF THE CORRECT ANSWER IN THE SPACE AT THE RIGHT.*

1. Which one of the following persons who has been injured in an accident should be the FIRST to be given first aid?

    A

    A. woman with a surface cut on her leg
    B. man with a sprained wrist
    C. man with a deep cut on the cheek which is bleeding profusely
    D. woman who complains that her- left hand feels broken

1.____

2. *Protection Agents are not allowed to read newspapers while on duty.*
    Which of the following is the MAIN reason for this rule?

    A. They may be distracted from their duties.
    B. They are not being paid to read newspapers.
    C. Such reading may lull them to sleep.
    D. Newspaper ink may come off on their hands.

2.____

3. The operator of a Transit Authority van hands Protection Agent Johnson a Material Pass listing the following: 31 boxes of No. 10 letter envelopes, 11 boxes - each containing 24 bottles of correction fluid, 18 packages of 14-inch photocopy paper, 12 packages of 11-inch photocopy paper, and 10 packages of paper towels. Agent Johnson counts the boxes and packages and finds a total of 79.
    How many boxes or packages are missing?

    A. 2   B. 3   C. 4   D. 5

3.____

4. *It is a violation of rules for a Protection Agent to carry a firearm while on Transit Authority property. The possession of such a weapon, whether carried on the person, in a personal vehicle, or stored in a locker, can result in charges being filed against the Agent.*
    According to the above information, the carrying of a firearm

    A. on Authority property by any employee is prohibited
    B. anywhere by an Agent is prohibited under all circumstances
    C. on Authority property by an Agent is prohibited under all circumstances
    D. anywhere by an Authority employee may be reason for charges being filed against that employee

4.____

5. *News reporters may enter Authority property if they have the written authorisation of a Public Affairs Department official. The Agent on duty must get permission from the Property Protection Control Desk before admitting to the property a news person who has no such written authorisation.*
    If a reporter tells a Protection Agent that she has received permission from the Authority President to enter the property, what is the FIRST thing the Agent should do?

5.____

A. Call the Authority police.
B. Admit the reporter immediately.
C. Call the Authority President's office.
D. Call the Property Protection Control Desk.

Questions 6-10.

DIRECTIONS: Questions 6 through 10 are to be answered SOLELY on the basis of the information in the paragraphs below titled FIRES AND EXTINGUISHERS.

FIRES AND EXTINGUISHERS

There are four classes of fires.

Trash fires, paper fires, cloth fires, wood fires, etc. are classified as Class A fires. Water or a water-base solution should be used to extinguish Class A fires. They also can be extinguished by covering the combustibles with a multi-purpose dry chemical.

Burning liquids, gasoline, oil, paint, tar, etc. are considered Class B fires. Such fires can be extinguished by smothering or blanketing them. Extinguishers used for Class B fires are Halon, CO_2, or multi-purpose dry chemical. Water tends to spread such fires and should not be used.

Fires in electrical equipment and switchboards are classified as Class C fires. When live electrical equipment is involved, a non-conducting extinguishing agent like CO_2, a multi-purpose dry chemical, or Halon should always be used. Soda-acid or other water-type extinguishers should not be used.

Class D fires consist of burning metals in finely-divided forms like chips, turnings, and shavings. Specially-designed extinguishing agents that provide a smothering blanket or coating should be used to extinguish Class D fires. Multi-purpose dry-powder extinguishants are such agents.

6. The ONLY type of extinguishing agent that can be used on any type of fire is   6._____

    A. a multi-purpose, dry-chemical, extinguishing agent
    B. soda-acid
    C. water
    D. carbon dioxide

7. A fire in litter swept from a subway car in a yard is MOST likely to be a Class _____ fire.   7._____

    A. A   B. B   C. C   D. D

8. Fire coming from the underbody of a subway car is MOST likely to be a Class _____   8._____
   fire.

    A. A   B. B   C. C   D. D

9. Which of the following extinguishing agents should NOT be used in fighting a Class C fire   9._____
   involving live electrical equipment?

    A. Halon
    B. CO_2

C. A multi-purpose dry chemical
D. Soda-acid

10. Water is NOT recommended for use on Class B fires because water   10.____

A. would cool the fire
B. evaporates too quickly
C. might spread the fire
D. would smother the fire

11. *An Officer on duty at a bus depot is required to have visitors sign a Visitor's Release form*   11.____
before admitting them to the property.
William Johnson, a tool manufacturer's representative, appears at the Ulmer Park bus
depot to keep an appointment with Supervisor Walter Minton. Harold Martin, the
Officer on duty, phones Mr. Minton, who tells him that he may admit Mr. Johnson. Mr.
Johnson, however, refuses to sign a Visitor's Release form.
Which of the following should Officer Martin do FIRST?

A. Call the Property Protection Control Desk.
B. Courteously explain to Mr. Johnson that rules require visitors to sign such forms
before they can be admitted.
C. Call Mr. Minton to tell him that Mr. Johnson refused to sign the release and that he
cannot admit him.
D. Call the Transit Police.

Questions 12-18.

DIRECTIONS: Questions 12 through 18 are to be answered SOLELY on the basis of the information given in the paragraph below and the Visitor's Release form.

On Friday, December 19, at 9:15 A.M., Joan Sanford, who represented the Adam
Hart Manufacturing Company, appeared at the Property Protection Agent booth at the 207th
Street, Manhattan, Main Shop. She stated that she wanted to see Superintendent Patterson
about a parts contract with her firm, which makes spare parts for subway cars. The Agent called
Mr. Patterson, who said he expected her. The Agent thereupon asked her to complete a Visitor's Release form, which she did. On the form, she indicated her age as 27, her occupation as
salesperson, her supervisor's name as Lawrence Austin, the firm's location at 1427 Cedar St.,
Glendale, N.Y., and her home address as 25-16 65th Road, Oak Point, N.Y. Agent Paul Jones
signed the Visitor's Release form as witness to her signature. She then entered the facility and
left Transit Authority property at 2 P.M., at which time Mr. Jones gave Miss Sanford a copy of the
Visitor's Release form.

Transit Authority   **VISITOR'S RELEASE**
The undersigned hereby agrees to hold harmless and indemnify The City of New York,
Metropolitan Transportation Authority, New York City Transit Authority, and their respective
members, officers, agents and employees, from any and all loss and liability for damages on
account of injuries (including death) to persons and damage to property attributable in whole or
in part to the negligence of the undersigned while on, or about the premises of the New York
City Transit Authority.

NYCTA Location to be visited: __1_____

_____

Duration of visit: From   _____ A.M.
                               _____ P.M.   _____ , 198__

                       To   _____ A.M.
                               _____ P.M.   _____ , 198__   } 2

Reason for visit: __3_____

_____

Age: __4_____   Occupation: __5_____

Firm represented: _____6_____

Employer: _____7_____

Address of Firm: _____8_____

Dated: _____9_____   (Signed) _____10_____

                                    Address _____11_____

                                    _____

Witness: _____12_____

(Two copies to be signed, one copy for NYCTA, one copy for visitor)

12. Which of the following should be on Line 4?   12.____

    A. 2 P.M.   B. 57
    C. 207th St. Shop   D. 27

13. Which of the following should be on Line 6?   13.____

    A. Joan Sanford
    B. Adam Hart Manufacturing Co.
    C. Oak Point Associates
    D. Patterson Manufacturing Co.

14. Which of the following should be on Line 11?   14.____

    A. 1427 Cedar St., Glendale, N.Y.
    B. 25-16 65th Road, Oak Point, N.Y.
    C. 3961 Tenth Ave., Manhattan, at 207th St.
    D. 26-15 65th Ave., Oak Point, N.Y.

15. Which of the following should be on Line 12?

    A. Miss Sanford's signature
    B. Mr. Patterson's signature
    C. Paul Jones' signature
    D. Lawrence Austin's name

15.____

16. On which of the following lines should *1427 Cedar St., Glendale, N.Y.* be entered?

    A. 2   B. 3   C. 7   D. 8

16.____

17. What is Miss Sanford's occupation?

    A. Superintendent   B. Protection Agent
    C. Salesperson   D. Manager, Sales

17.____

18. Which of the following should be entered in Section 2 of the form?

    A. 9:00 A.M. and 2:00 P.M.   B. 9:15 A.M. and 2:00 P.M.
    C. 9:15 A.M. and 2:15 P.M.   D. 9:15 A.M. and 3:00 P.M.

18.____

19. Six employees drive six passenger cars with Transit Authority decals into the Jamaica Yard parking lot after displaying their passes to the Agent. An hour later, two of those employees drive two of the cars out of the lot. Ten minutes later, two of those employees leave in one of the cars. A half hour after that, the other two employees leave in one of the cars with three other employees seated in the back.
How many of the six cars that entered together remain in the lot?

    A. 1   B. 2   C. 3   D. 4

19.____

20. *All unusual occurrences and hazards should be reported promptly to the Property Protection Control Desk.*
A person on the street throws a rock through the window of the Protection Agent's booth at a train yard, shattering the glass but not causing personal injury. The FIRST action the Protection Agent should take is to

    A. run out to the street and attempt to apprehend the rock thrower
    B. call the Property Protection Control Desk and report the incident
    C. sweep up the broken glass so that no one will step on it
    D. pick up the rock and throw it at the culprit to halt him so he may be apprehended

20.____

Questions 21-24.

DIRECTIONS: Questions 21 through 24 are to be answered SOLELY on the basis of the following information.
    Under Transit Authority and Property Protection Department rules, only authorized visitors and employees with Authority passes may enter a Transit Authority facility.

21. A woman not employed by the Transit Authority asks a Protection Agent at the East 180th St. train yard whether she may use the yard's ladies room.
The Protection Agent should tell her that

    A. she may if she takes no longer than 10 minutes
    B. she must first ask the location chief whether she may use that facility

21.____

C.   she may do so only if she is related to an employee assigned to the yard
D.   he is sorry but Transit Authority rules prohibit her admittance

22.   A boy involved in a softball game on a lot next to a bus depot parking lot tells a Protection   22.____
Agent that one of the batters hit a pitch over the fence and into the Transit Authority lot.
He asks permission to retrieve the ball.
Which of the following is the BEST course of action for the Protection Agent?
He should

   A.   permit the boy to go onto the lot to retrieve the ball
   B.   tell the boy that he may not go onto the lot, but that he can claim the ball at the
        Transit Authority's Lost Property Office
   C.   tell the boy to wait at the gate until he (the Protection Agent) retrieves the ball and
        returns it to him
   D.   tell the boy that he must leave the ball where it landed and that he and his friends
        must discontinue playing ball so close to the depot parking lot

23.   Car Inspector Boggs, employed at the Pitkin Train Yard, calls Agent Hernandez, sta-   23.____
tioned at an entrance of the train yard, to tell him that his wife, Helen Boggs, is coming to
the facility to pick up a personal article from him.
Agent Hernandez should tell Mr. Boggs that

   A.   he will have to wait until he returns home to give her the article
   B.   he is not permitted to have visitors at the train yard while he is working
   C.   he, Agent Hernandez, will call him when his wife arrives and that he must come to
        the booth to see her
   D.   he will send Mrs. Boggs inside to see him

24.   A woman with a briefcase enters the lobby at Transit Authority headquarters and is   24.____
stopped by a Protection Agent assigned there. She says she represents the Fail Safe
Brush Company and wants to offer brushes and other home-cleaning products for sale to
Transit Authority employees.
The Agent should politely tell her that

   A.   she may go to the various floors for that purpose so long as she does not disturb
        employees while they are working
   B.   she first must go to the executive floor to ask the Senior Vice President for permis-
        sion to solicit employees
   C.   she may not enter the building to sell products to Transit Authority employees
   D.   if she wishes she may stand in the lobby and solicit employees as they enter or
        leave the building

25.   A Protection Agent on duty at the Jerome Avenue Yard opened the vehicle gate at 2:29   25.____
A.M. to allow employee cars with decal numbers 526 and 495 to enter. The car with
decal No. 495 was driven out of the yard after having been inside for 37 minutes. The car
with decal No. 526 left the yard one hour and 18 minutes after car No. 495.
At what time did car No. 526 leave the yard?

   A.   3:06 A.M.   B.   4:06 A.M.
   C.   4:24 A.M.   D.   4:24 P.M.

Questions 26-29.

DIRECTIONS: Questions 26 through 29 are to be answered SOLELY on the basis of the information in the paragraph below.

Protection Agent Brown, working the midnight-to-8:00 A.M. tour at the Flushing Bus Depot, discovered a fire at 2:17 A.M. in Bus No. 4651, which was parked in the southeast portion of the depot yard. He turned in an alarm to the Fire Department from Box 3297 on the nearby street at 2:18 A.M. At 2:20 A.M., he called the Property Protection Control Desk and reported the fire and his action to Line Supervisor Wilson. Line Supervisor Wilson instructed Agent Brown to lock his booth and go to the fire alarm box to direct the fire companies. The first arriving companies were Engine 307 and Ladder 154. Brown directed them to the burning bus. Two minutes later, at 2:23 A.M., Battalion Chief Welsh arrived from Battalion 14. The fire had made little headway. It was extinguished in about two minutes. Brown then wrote a fire report for submittal to Line Supervisor Wilson.

26. What was the FIRST thing Protection Agent Brown did after observing the fire? 26._____
    He

    A. called Battalion Chief Welsh
    B. called the Fire Dispatcher
    C. transmitted an alarm from a nearby alarm box
    D. called 911

27. In what part of the yard was the burning bus? 27._____
    The

    A. northeast section   B. southwest end
    C. northwest part   D. southeast portion

28. What time did Agent Brown call Line Supervisor Wilson? 28._____

    A. 2:18 PM   B. 2:20 AM   C. 2:29 AM   D. 2:36 AM

29. Which of the following CORRECTLY describes the sequence of Agent Brown's actions? 29._____
    He

    A. saw the fire, turned in an alarm, called the Property Protection Control Desk, directed the fire companies to the fire, and wrote a report
    B. called the Property Protection Control Desk, directed the fire apparatus, directed Chief Welsh, and wrote
    C. a report
    D. called Line Supervisor Wilson, turned in an alarm, waited by the burning bus, and directed the fire companies
    E. called Line Supervisor Wilson, directed the fire fighters, waited for instructions from Line Supervisor Wilson, and wrote a report

Questions 30-31.

DIRECTIONS: Questions 30 and 31 are to be answered SOLELY on the basis of the following paragraph and rule.

Protection Agents may admit to Transit Authority headquarters only persons with Transit Authority passes, persons with job appointment letters, and persons who have permission to enter from Transit Authority officials.

During his tour in the Authority's headquarters lobby, Protection Agent Williams admitted to the building 326 persons with Authority passes and 41 persons with job appointment letters. He telephoned authorized officials for permission to admit 14 others, 13 of whom were granted permission and entered and one of whom was denied permission. He also turned away two persons who wanted to enter to sell to employees merchandise for their personal use, and one person who appeared inebriated.

30. How many persons did Agent Williams admit to the building?   30.____

    A. 326   B. 367   C. 380   D. 382

31. To how many persons did Agent Williams refuse admittance?   31.____

    A. 4   B. 13   C. 14   D. 41

Questions 32-35.

DIRECTIONS: Questions 32 through 35 are to be answered SOLELY on the basis of the information in the following paragraph.

On Tuesday, October 21, Protection Agent Williams, on duty at the Jamaica Depot, observed a man jump over the fence and into the parking lot at 2:12 P.M. and run to a car that was parked with the engine running. The man, who limped slightly, opened the car door, jumped into the car, and sped, out of the yard. The car was a 1991 gray Buick Electra, license plate 563-JYN, with parking decal No. 6043. The man was white, about 6 feet tall, about 175 pounds, in his mid-20's, with a scar on his left cheek. He wore a blue sportcoat, tan slacks, a white shirt open at the neck with no tie, and brown loafers.

32. What was the color of the car?   32.____

    A. White   B. Blue
    C. Two-tone brown and tan   D. Gray

33. What were the distinguishing personal features of the man who jumped over the fence?   33.____

    A. A scar on the left cheek
    B. Pockmarks on his face
    C. A cast on his left wrist
    D. Bushy eyebrows

34. What was the number on the car's parking decal?   34.____

    A. 1991   B. 673-JYN   C. 6043   D. 175

35. On what day of the week did the incident occur?   35.____

    A. Monday   B. Tuesday   C. Wednesday   D. Sunday

KEY (CORRECT ANSWERS)

1.	C		16.	D
2.	A		17.	C
3.	B		18.	B
4.	C		19.	B
5.	D		20.	B
6.	A		21.	D
7.	A		22.	C
8.	C		23.	C
9.	D		24.	C
10.	C		25.	C
11.	B		26.	C
12.	D		27.	D
13.	B		28.	B
14.	B		29.	A
15.	C		30.	C

31.	A
32.	D
33.	A
34.	C
35.	B

TEST 2

Questions 1-10.

DIRECTIONS Questions 1 through 10 are to be answered SOLELY on the basis of the information in the paragraphs below titled SCRAP TRANSFER and the Record of Scrap Award form.

SCRAP TRANSFER

Protection Agent Robert Green, Pass No. 104123, was assigned to Post 27A at the main entrance of the Fifth Ave., Brooklyn Train Yard on Thursday, October 23, on the 8 A.M.-to-4 P.M. tour. At 10:10 A.M., a scrap removal truck, No. 64, license plate AB-4126, from the J.H. Trucking Company stopped at the gate. The driver showed Agent Green a scrap contract with Award No. 1626 for the removal of 12 headlamps from this location.

Agent Green called Supervisor Raymond Hadley in Storeroom 18 for verification of the award. Supervisor Hadley verified the award. The driver then proceeded to Storeroom 18, where he loaded the headlamps into the truck. Hadley then made out a Materials Permit, signed it, and placed his pass number (521800) on it, and gave it to the driver. At the gate, the driver presented the Materials Permit to Agent Green, who logged out the truck at 10:40 A.M., whereupon the truck left for its destination in the Bronx.

Agent Green transcribed the information on his registry sheet and the Materials Permit to a Record of Scrap Award form, which he handed to Line Supervisor Brian Sullivan (Pass No. 756349), who had just arrived at the post. Line Supervisor Sullivan, after having checked the form carefully, signed it and wrote his pass number on it.

RECORD OF SCRAP AWARD

DATE _____1_____

POST NO. _____2_____ TOUR _____3_____

NAME OF CARRIER _____4_____ AWARD NO. _____5_____

TRUCK LICENSE NO. _____6_____

TRUCK NO. _____7_____

DESTINATION _____8_____

TIME IN _____9_____ TIME OUT _____10_____

DESCRIPTION OF SCRAP _____11_____

AMOUNT _____12_____

NAME OF SUPERVISOR OR DESIGNEE _____13_____

PASS NUMBER _____

_____14_____
TRANSIT PROPERTY PROTECTION AGENT

_____15_____
PASS NO.

_____16_____
LINE SUPERVISOR (SIGNATURE)

_____17_____
PASS NO.

1. Which of the following should be on Line 2? 1.____

A. 27A B. Coney Island
C. Storeroom 18 D. Main gate

2. Which of the following should be on Line 3? 2.____

A. 12 Midnight - 8 A.M. B. 12 P.M. - 8 P.M.
C. 8 A.M. - 4 P.M. D. 4 P.M. - 12 P.M.

3. Which of the following should be on Line 4? 3.____

A. J.H. Trucking Co. B. Line Supervisor Sullivan
C. Transit Authority D. Storeroom 18

4. Which of the following should be on Line 8? 4.____

A. Fifth Ave. Yard B. Bronx, N.Y.
C. Storeroom 18 D. Post 27A

5. Which of the following should be on Line 10? 5.____

A. 9:10 A.M. B. 10:10 A.M.
C. 10:30 A.M. D. 10:40 A.M.

25

6. Which of the following should be on Line 16?
   _____ signature.

   A. Robert Green's   B. Brian Sullivan's
   C. the truck driver's   D. Raymond Hadley's

7. On which of the following lines should *104123* be entered?

   A. 10   B. 12   C. 15   D. 17

8. On which of the following lines should *AB4216* be entered?

   A. 1   B. 3   C. 6   D. 13

9. On which of the following lines should *12 headlamps* be entered?

   A. 3   B. 11   C. 14   D. 17

10. On which of the following lines should 10:10 A.M. be entered?

   A. 8   B. 9   C. 10   D. 11

Questions 11-15.

DIRECTIONS: Questions 11 through 15 are to be answered SOLELY on the basis of the infor-
             mation in the KEY STATIONS DIRECTORY below. Key Stations are locations
             which Protection Agents must visit and inspect on their hourly rounds.

KEY STATIONS DIRECTORY

Key Station No. 1 - Protection Agent's booth at Flushing Train Yard
Key Station No. 2 - On parking lot fence adjacent to No. 4 track
Key Station No. 3 - On stairwell No. 8 in the Boiler Room
Key Station No. 4 - On the door leading to the second floor men's locker room
Key Station No. 5 - Alongside the soda machine in the second floor lunchroom
Key Station No. 6 - On the oilhouse door
Key Station No. 7 - Alongside the bulletin board in the main shop
Key Station No. 8 - Next to fire extinguisher No. 12 on the wall to the left of the entrance to
                      the Supervisor's office
Key Station No. 9 - On the bumper block of Track No. 10

11. The number of the key station near the main shop bulletin board is

   A. 5   B. 6   C. 7   D. 8

12. Where is Key Station No. 4?

   A. On the parking lot fence adjacent to Track 4
   B. On the door of the second floor men's locker room
   C. On the oilhouse door
   D. In the second floor lunchroom

13. The number of the key station in the Protection Agent's booth is

   A. 1   B. 3   C. 7   D. 9

14. No. 5 Key Station is located

    A. next to fire extinguisher No. 6 in the Protection Agent's booth
    B. on the bumper block of Track 10
    C. in the second floor lunchroom next to the soda machine
    D. on the parking lot fence near Track No. 4

14.____

15. The number of the key station on the parking lot fence adjacent to Track No. 4 is

    A. 1   B. 2   C. 3   D. 8

15.____

Questions 16-18.

DIRECTIONS: Questions 16 through 18 are to be answered SOLELY on the basis of the following rule.
A Protection Agent must remain on his post (assigned area) during his entire tour.

16. In order to have lunch, a Protection Agent should

    A. go to the nearest restaurant and eat his lunch quickly
    B. bring his lunch or have another person get his lunch for him
    C. go to his locker room to have a brief lunch
    D. telephone the Property Protection Control Desk to inform the supervisor that he is going for a short lunch break

16.____

17. While on duty at a train yard, a Protection Agent discovers that his flashlight, one of the items he is required to have in his possession while he is working, is inoperable.
Which of the following is his BEST course of action?

    A. Go to the nearest hardware store, buy new batteries, a new bulb, or a new flashlight and obtain a receipt.
    B. Go to the location chief's office and borrow a flashlight from an Agent assigned to that office.
    C. Make out a written report stating that the flashlight does not work.
    D. Call the Property Protection Control Desk for a replacement flashlight.

17.____

18. A woman in a third floor apartment across the street from a Transit Authority bus depot is standing at the window screaming that her apartment is on fire.
The Protection Agent assigned to the depot, seeing flames behind the woman, should IMMEDIATELY

    A. telephone the Fire Department
    B. lock his booth and rush into the building to rescue the woman
    C. take his fire extinguisher and rush to the apartment to extinguish the flames
    D. run across the street, stand under the window, and call to the woman to jump into his arms

18.____

19. Registry Sheets must be filled in by Protection Agents assigned to bus depots, train yards, and certain other Transit Authority locations. A Protection Agent must enter on a Registry Sheet the name and pass number or firm name and address, whichever applies, of each person entering with the time in and time out. For a vehicle, he must enter the vehicle number - if a Transit Authority vehicle, the decal or license number of the vehicle, time in and time out, and the destinations of occupants. Each person enter

19.____

ing must sign the Registry Sheet, with the exceptions of Transit Authority Special Inspectors and police officers, who nevertheless must identify themselves to the Protection Agent on duty. The Protection Agent must record the name of the police officer or Special Inspector, his shield number, time of arrival and departure, and car number if the officer or Inspector drove a car onto the property.

If a Transit Authority detective in civilian clothes enters the property, the Protection Agent must

    A.   allow him to enter the property without asking any questions
    B.   make sure the detective displays his credentials so that the Protection Agent may record his name, shield number, and time of arrival
    C.   request the detective to write his name, shield number, and signature upon the Registry Sheet
    D.   immediately call the location chief to notify him that the detective has been admitted to make an investigation

Questions 20-21.

DIRECTIONS: Questions 20 and 21 are to be answered SOLELY on the basis of the following portion of a rule.

...in the event that a claim is made at a place where a lost article is being held pending transmittal to the Lost Property Office and identification is made to the satisfaction of the employee in charge, such employee may, upon receiving permission from the proper authority, deliver such article to the owner, taking a receipt therefor upon the form prescribed...

20.   A Protection Agent at the Flushing bus depot parking lot finds a pair of eyeglasses in a case. Shortly thereafter, a Transit Authority employee states that he dropped the eyeglasses and that his name and address are in the case. He identifies himself and the Protection Agent finds his name and address in the case. A Line Supervisor tells the Protection Agent to have the employee sign a receipt form for the glasses.
What action should the Protection Agent then take?   20.____

    A.   He should tell the employee to try on the glasses and read a sign across the street and a memorandum in small type to prove the glasses are his.
    B.   He should call the man's supervisor and ask him whether he has seen the employee wearing the glasses the Protection Agent describes.
    C.   He should immediately give the employee the glasses and allow him to leave with them.
    D.   He should instruct the employee to sign a receipt form and, after he does so, he should give the employee the glasses.

21.   Conductor Alvin Bell finds a briefcase on an *A* train in Brooklyn. He takes it to headquarters at 370 Jay Street at 7:25 P.M. Agent James Norton, on duty there, tells him the Lost Property Office is open only from 8:30 A.M. to 4:30 P.M. Mondays to Fridays. At that moment, a woman enters the lobby and tells Agent Norton that she left a briefcase which contains her name and address and valuable papers on an *A* train. Agent Norton tells her that she will have to return the next business day between 8:30 A.M. and 4:30 P.M. to the Lost Property Office to identify the briefcase.
The information Protection Agent Norton gave the woman was   21.____

A. *incorrect* because he should have taken her word for it and should have given her the briefcase immediately

B. *correct* because it might not have been her briefcase

C. *incorrect* because he should have given her the briefcase, with supervisory approval, if she would have identified herself, correctly described the contents of the briefcase, and signed the required receipt

D. *correct* because lost property may be redeemed only at the Lost Property Office

22. *All Protection Agents are required to phone the Property Protection Control Desk between 20 and 40 minutes after the hour, except during the first and last hours of their tours when they are not required to phone in.*
Agent Jane Simlowicz is assigned to Post 14C at the Flushing Train Yard from 8:00 A.M. to 4:00 P.M.
Which of the following times would be appropriate for her to make her first call to the Property Protection Control Desk?

    A. 8:35 AM   B. 9:35 AM   C. 9:50 AM   D. 10:45 AM

22.____

23. *The playing of musical instruments on Transit Authority property is forbidden.*
During his lunch period, a Transit Authority employee begins playing a bagpipe in a bus depot parking lot to practice his part with a Transit Authority contingent in the Saint Patrick's Day Parade.
The Protection Agent on duty should tell the employee to

A. play the bagpipe softly at the far end of the parking lot

B. return to the garage to get his supervisor's permission to practice on the bagpipe in the parking lot

C. enter a bus parked in the lot, close the doors, and play the bagpipe so it cannot be heard outside

D. stop playing the bagpipe

23.____

24. Agent Fitzgerald, on duty at the bus depot, observes a woman employee come out of the bus garage and enter a car parked on the depot's lot. The car bursts into flames when she turns the ignition key.
The FIRST thing Agent Fitzgerald should consider doing is to

A. run to the nearest fire alarm box and transmit an alarm

B. call the Property Protection Control Desk and ask a supervisor to summon the Fire Department

C. run to the car and try to open the door and pull the woman to safety

D. rush into the depot, get a pail of water, and throw the water onto the burning car

24.____

25. *Telephones in Transit Authority buildings and in other Transit Authority facilities are solely for the business of the Transit Authority.*
A man enters the lobby of the Transit Authority building at 25 Chapel Street and tells the Agent on duty that his car has been struck by another vehicle and that he wants to telephone for a tow truck.
The Agent should tell him that

A. he may go to one of the upper floors and ask a Transit Authority employee whether he may use that employee's telephone

B. he should go to the corner of Jay Street and use the police emergency telephone that is on the lamppost

25.____

C. he is sorry but all Transit Authority telephones are for Transit Authority business calls only

D. he, the Protection Agent, will call 911 and ask the police to send a tow truck

Questions 26-30.

DIRECTIONS: Questions 26 through 30 are to be answered SOLELY on the basis of the information in the following table.

ASSIGNMENTS FOR THE WEEK OF OCTOBER 19

Title & Name	Post	Tour	Off
Protection Agent John Hall	2B	5 PM - 1 AM	Tues. & Wed.
Protection Agent William Ball	10A	8 AM - 4 PM	Thurs. & Fri.
Protection Agent Robert Hale	4A	4 PM - 12 PM	Sat. & Sun.
Protection Agent Sandra Hill	3B	12 PM - 8 AM	Fri. & Sat.
Protection Agent Brenda Wall	11C	7 PM - 3 AM	Wed. & Thurs.

26. The tour of 4 P.M. to Midnight with Friday and Saturday off is worked by   26._____

    A. Robert Hale   B. Brenda Wall
    C. William Ball   D. none of the Agents

27. Which Agent has Saturday and Sunday off?   27._____

    A. John Hall   B. Robert Hale
    C. Brenda Wall   D. Sandra Hill

28. What day of the week do all the Agents work?   28._____

    A. Monday   B. Wednesday   C. Thursday   D. Sunday

29. Which of the Agents are off on Wednesday?   29._____

    A. Ball and Wall   B. Hall and Hale
    C. Wall and Hall   D. Hill and Ball

30. Which of the Agents works Saturday through Wednesday?   30._____

    A. Sandra Hill   B. John Hall
    C. William Ball   D. Brenda Wall

31. *Only authorized employees are permitted to enter a Protection Agent's booth.*   31._____
A woman with a boy about 4 years old approaches the Agent on duty at the 207th St. Yard on Easter Sunday and asks whether she may leave her son in the booth for about a half hour while she visits a seriously ill bedridden friend across the street. The Agent should tell her

    A. that since her son is not an authorized employee, he cannot enter the booth
    B. the boy may sit in the booth for no longer than a half hour so long as he is quiet and does not touch any property
    C. she should take the boy to the nearest police precinct and pick him up upon her return
    D. she should take the boy to a day care center where experienced children's counselors will care for him

32. While on duty at the Jamaica Yard, Agent Barbara McCoy sees a man fall in the yard and   32.____
lie motionless, apparently the victim of a heart attack.
Which of the following actions should she take FIRST?

    A.   Lift the man and take him into the Protection Agent's booth.
    B.   Write a report of an unusual occurrence.
    C.   Call 911 and ask for an ambulance.
    D.   Go to the yard supervisor and ask him to assign personnel to drive the man to a hospital.

33. *Employees are prohibited from possessing or drinking alcoholic beverages on Transit*   33.____
Authority property.
An Authority employee assigned to the 207th St. Main Shop is about to retire, and his
co-workers have planned a farewell party. Some buy food, soda, coffee, and tea at a
nearby supermarket and take it into the yard. Agent Simmons, on duty at the entrance
booth, inspects their bundles and allows them to enter. Another of the retiree's co-
workers carries a bag containing a bottle of Scotch and a bottle of rye.
Agent Simmons, after inspecting the bag, should tell him

    A.   to make sure that none of the contents are spilled on the floor of the party room
    B.   to make sure that neither of the bottles get broken
    C.   to make sure that the empty bottles and other trash are disposed of properly
    D.   that he cannot take the contents of the bag onto Authority property

34. *Transit Authority employees are required to present a Materials Pass before being per-*   34.____
mitted to take any Authority material or personal property from Transit Authority property.
James Thompson, a Farebox Maintainer, is carrying a package as he exits from his
work location. The Agent on duty asks him for a Materials Pass. Mr. Thompson opens
the package and displays a large box of cigars. What action should the Protection
Agent take?
He should

    A.   allow the employee to leave with the cigars since they are not Transit Authority material
    B.   call Mr. Thompson's supervisor to ask whether Mr. Thompson may take the cigars with him
    C.   tell Mr. Thompson that he may take the cigars with him only if he produces a sales slip for them
    D.   explain to Mr. Thompson that he must obtain a Materials Pass before he can take the package out of the facility

35. *Each Protection Agent who is assigned to a post where a watchclock is required must*   35.____
take every precaution to protect the watchclock from damage and theft. It must never be
dropped or abused in any way. The Agent is held strictly accountable for any damage to
the clock during his tour. Therefore, he must examine the clock and its case carefully in
the presence of the Agent he relieves and report any irregularity immediately to the Prop-
erty Protection Control Desk.
If, upon arrival for duty, a Protection Agent finds that the watchclock has been dam-
aged, his FIRST action should be to

31

A. accept full responsibility for the damage
B. lock up the watchclock as a precaution against theft
C. report the finding to the Property Protection Control Desk
D. tell the Agent on duty that he cannot relieve him because he has apparently dropped or abused the watchclock

---

KEY (CORRECT ANSWERS)

1.	A		16.	B
2.	C		17.	D
3.	A		18.	A
4.	B		19.	B
5.	D		20.	D
6.	B		21.	C
7.	C		22.	B
8.	C		23.	D
9.	B		24.	C
10.	B		25.	C
11.	C		26.	D
12.	B		27.	B
13.	A		28.	A
14.	C		29.	C
15.	B		30.	C

31.	A
32.	C
33.	D
34.	D
35.	C

WRITTEN ENGLISH EXPRESSION

EXAMINATION SECTION
TEST 1

Questions 1-5.

DIRECTIONS: Each of the following sentences may be classified under one of the following four categories:
  A. faulty because of incorrect grammar
  B. faulty because of incorrect punctuation
  C. faulty because of incorrect capitalization or incorrect spelling
  D. correct
  Examine each sentence carefully. Then, in the space at the right, print the letter preceding the option which is best of those suggested above. All incorrect sentences contain but one type of error. Consider a sentence correct if it contains none of the types of errors mentioned, even though there may be other correct ways of expressing the same thought.

1. They told both he and I that the prisoner had escaped.   1.____

2. Any superior officer, who, disregards the just complaints of his subordinates, is remiss in   2.____
   the performance of his duty.

3. Only those members of the national organization who resided in the Middle West   3.____
   attended the conference in Chicago.

4. We told him to give the investigation assignment to whoever was available.   4.____

5. Please do not disappoint and embarass us by not appearing in court.   5.____

Questions 6-10.

DIRECTIONS: Each of the following sentences may be classified under one of the following four categories:
  A. faulty because of incorrect spelling only
  B. faulty because of incorrect grammar or word usage only
  C. faulty because of one error in spelling and one error in grammar or word usage
  D. correct
  Examine each sentence carefully. Then, in the space at the right, print the letter preceding the option which is best of those suggested above. All incorrect sentences contain but one type of error. Consider a sentence correct if it contains none of the types of errors mentioned, even though there may be other correct ways of expressing the same thought.

6. Although the officer's speech proved to be entertaining, the topic was not relevant to the   6.____
   main theme of the conference.

7. In February all new officers attended a training course in which they were learned their principal duties and the fundamental operating procedures of the department.

7.____

8. I personally seen inmate Jones threaten inmates Smith and Green with bodily harm if they refused to participate in the plot.

8.____

9. To the layman, who on a chance visit to the prison observes everything functioning smoothly, the maintenance of prison discipline may seem to be a relatively easily realizable objective.

9.____

10. The prisoners in cell block fourty were forbidden to lay on the cell cots during the recreation hour.

10.____

Questions 11-22.

DIRECTIONS: Each of the following sentences may be classified under one of the following four categories:
   A. faulty because of incorrect grammar
   B. faulty because of incorrect punctuation
   C. faulty because of incorrect capitalization or incorrect spelling
   D. correct
Examine each sentence carefully. Then, in the space at the right, print the letter preceding the option which is best of those suggested above. All incorrect sentences contain but one type of error. Consider a sentence correct if it contains none of the types of errors mentioned, even though there may be other correct ways of expressing the same thought.

11. I cannot encourage you any.

11.____

12. You always look well in those sort of clothes.

12.____

13. Shall we go to the park?

13.____

14. The man whome he introduced was Mr. Carey.

14.____

15. She saw the letter laying here this morning.

15.____

16. It should rain before the Afternoon is over.

16.____

17. They have already went home.

17.____

18. That Jackson will be elected is evident.

18.____

19. He does not hardly approve of us.

19.____

20. It was he, who won the prize.

20.____

21. Shall we go to the park.

21.____

22. They are, alike, in this particular.

22.____

———

KEY (CORRECT ANSWERS)

1.	A	11.	A
2.	B	12.	A
3.	C	13.	D
4.	D	14.	C
5.	C	15.	A
6.	A	16.	C
7.	C	17.	A
8.	B	18.	D
9.	D	19.	A
10.	C	20.	B

21. B
22. B

TEST 2

DIRECTIONS: Among the sentences in this test are some which cannot be accepted in formal, written English for one or another of the following reasons:

POOR DICTION: The use of a word which is improper either because its meaning does not fit the sentence or because it is not acceptable in formal writing.
Example;   The audience was strongly <u>effected</u> by the senator's speech.

VERBOSITY: Repetitious elements adding nothing to the meaning of the sentence and not justified by any need for special emphasis.
Example: At that time there was <u>then</u> no right of petition.

FAULTY GRAMMAR: Word forms and expressions which do not conform to the grammatical and structural usages required by formal written English (errors in case, number, parallelism, and the like).
Example;   Everyone in the delegation had <u>their</u> reasons for opposing the measure.

No sentence has more than one kind of error. Some sentences have no errors. Read each sentence carefully; then, in the space at the right, print the letter:
   D if the sentence contains an error in <u>diction</u>
   V if the sentence is <u>verbose</u>
   G if the sentence contains <u>faulty grammar</u>
   O if the sentence contains <u>none</u> of these errors.

1.   I will not go unless I receive a special invitation.   1._____

2.   The pilot shouted decisive orders to his assistant as the plane burst into flames.   2._____

3.   She acts like her feelings were hurt.   3._____

4.   Please come here and try and help me finish this piece of work.   4._____

5.   As long as you are ready, you may as well start promptly and on time.   5._____

6.   My younger brother insists that he is as tall as me.   6._____

7.   A spiritual person is usually deeply concerned with mundane affairs.   7._____

8.   Speaking from practical experience, I advise you to give up those unquestionably quixotic schemes.   8._____

9.   We walked as long as there was any light to guide us.   9._____

10.   Realizing I had forgotten my gloves, I returned to the theatre, using a flashlight and turned down every seat.   10._____

11.   The winters were hard and dreary, nothing could live without shelter.   11._____

12.   Not one in a thousand readers take the matter seriously.   12._____

13. This tire has so many defections that it is worthless.   13._____

14. The jury were divided in their views.   14._____

15. He was so credulous that his friends found it hard to deceive him.   15._____

16. The emperor's latest ukase is sure to stir up such resentment that the people will revolt. 16._____

17. When you go to the library tomorrow, please bring this book to the librarian in the reference room.   17._____

18. His speech is so precise as to seem infected.   18._____

19. I had sooner serve overseas before I remain inactive at home.   19._____

20. We read each other's letters together.   20._____

KEY (CORRECT ANSWERS)

1. O
2. V   Eliminate <u>decisive</u>
3. G   Use *as though* instead of <u>like</u>
4. V   Eliminate <u>and try</u>
5. V   Eliminate <u>and on time</u>

6. G   *I* instead of <u>me</u>
7. D   <u>Mundane</u> means worldly; what is needed here is *religious* or *ethereal*
8. O
9. O
10. G   To achieve parallelism and balance, rewrite as follows: "*...and, using a flashlight, turned down every seat.*"
11. G   Semicolon (;) after <u>dreary</u> instead of comma (,)
12. G   *Takes*, not <u>take</u>
13. D   *Defects*, not <u>defections</u>
14. O
15. D   *Easy*, not <u>hard</u>
16. O
17. D   *Take*, not <u>bring</u>
18. D   *Affected*, not <u>infected</u>
19. G   Replace <u>before I</u> by *than*
20. V   Eliminate *together*

TEST 3

DIRECTIONS: Among the sentences in this test are some which cannot be accepted in formal, written English for one or another of the following reasons:

POOR DICTION: The use of a word which is improper either because its meaning does not fit the sentence or because it is not acceptable in formal writing.
Example: The audience was strongly <u>effected</u> by the senator's speech.

VERBOSITY: Repetitious elements adding nothing to the meaning of the sentence and not justified by any need for special emphasis.
Example: At that time there was <u>then</u> no right of petition.

FAULTY GRAMMAR: Word forms and expressions which do not conform to the grammatical and structural usages required by formal written English (errors in case, number, parallelism, and the like).
Example: Everyone in the delegation had <u>their</u> reasons for opposing the measure.

No sentence has more than one kind of error. Some sentences have no errors. Read each sentence carefully; then, in the space at the right, print the letter:
    D if the sentence contains an error in <u>diction</u>
    V if the sentence is <u>verbose</u>
    G if the sentence contains <u>faulty grammar</u>
    O if the sentence contains <u>none</u> of these errors.

1.   Choose an author as you choose a friend.   1.____

2.   Home is home, be it ever so humble and so plain.   2.____

3.   Invidious smokers usually find it difficult to break the habit.   3.____

4.   You always look devastating in that sort of clothes.   4.____

5.   We had no sooner entered the room when the bell rang.   5.____

6.   A box of choice figs was sent him for Christmas.   6.____

7.   Neither Charles or his brother finished his assignment.   7.____

8.   There goes the last piece of cake and the last spoonful of ice cream.   8.____

9.   Diamonds are more desired than any precious stones.   9.____

10.   The administrator's unconscionable demands elated the workers.   10.____

11.   Never before, to the best of my recollection, has there been such promising students.   11.____

12.   It is only because your manners are so objectionable that you are not invited to the party.   12.____

13.   An altruistic proverb is: "God helps those who help themselves."   13.____

14. I fully expected that the children would be at their desks and to find them ready to begin work.   14.____

15. A complete system of railroads covers and crisscrosses the entire country.   15.____

16. Our vacation being over, I am sorry to say.   16.____

17. It is so dark that I can't hardly see.   17.____

18. Either you or I am right; we cannot both be right.   18.____

19. After it had laid in the rain all night, it was not fit for use again.   19.____

20. Although the meaning was implicit, the statement required further explanation.   20.____

KEY (CORRECT ANSWERS)

1. O
2. V   Eliminate and so plain
3. D   *Inveterate*, not invidious
4. D   *Well*, not devastating
5. G   *Than*, for well
6. O
7. G   *Nor*, for or
8. G   *Go*, for goes
9. G   Insert *other* after any
10. D   *Embittered*, not elated
11. G   *Have*, not has
12. O
13. D   Not altruistic, *selfish*
14. G   To assure parallelism and balance, place comma (,) after desks, and eliminate and to find them
15. V   Eliminate and crisscrosses
16. G   Replace being by *is*
17. G   *Can hardly see*, not can't hardly see
18. O
19. D, G   *Lain*, not laid
20. O

TEST 4

DIRECTIONS: Among the sentences in this test are some which cannot be accepted in formal, written English for one or another of the following reasons:

POOR DICTION: The use of a word which is improper either because its meaning does not fit the sentence or because it is not acceptable in formal writing.
Example: The audience was strongly <u>effected</u> by the senator's speech.

VERBOSITY: Repetitious elements adding nothing to the meaning of the sentence and not justified by any need for special emphasis.
Example: At that time there was <u>then</u> no right of petition.

FAULTY GRAMMAR: Word forms and expressions which do not conform to the grammatical and structural usages required by formal written English (errors in case, number, parallelism, and the like).
Example: Everyone in the delegation had <u>their</u> reasons for opposing the measure.

No sentence has more than one kind of error. Some sentences have no errors. Read each sentence carefully; then, in the space at the right, print the letter:
    D if the sentence contains an error in <u>diction</u>
    V if the sentence is <u>verbose</u>
    G if the sentence contains <u>faulty grammar</u>
    O if the sentence contains <u>none</u> of these errors

1. Neither Tom nor John were present for the rehearsal.   1._____

2. She admired the cavalier manner with which her husband treated her.   2._____

3. The happiness or misery of men's lives depend on their early training.   3._____

4. Honor as well as profit are to be gained by those studies.   4._____

5. The egg business is only incidental to the regular business of the general store.   5._____

6. It was superior in every way to the book previously read.   6._____

7. We found his captious suggestions to be friendly and constructive.   7._____

8. His testimony today is completely and radically different from that of yesterday.   8._____

9. If you would have studied the problem carefully you would have found the solution more quickly.   9._____

10. The large tips he received made the job a highly lucid one despite its long hours.   10._____

11. The flowers smelled so sweet that the whole house was perfumed.   11._____

12. When either or both habits becomes fixed, the student improves.   12._____

13. Neither his words nor his action were justifiable.   13._____

14. A calm almost always comes before a storm.   14.____

15. The gallery with all its pictures were destroyed.   15.____

16. Those trees which are not deciduous remain green and attractive all winter.   16.____

17. Whom did they say won?   17.____

18. The man whom I thought was my friend deceived me.   18.____

19. Send whoever will do the work.   19.____

20. The question of who should be leader arose and the power he should have.   20.____

KEY (CORRECT ANSWERS)

1.	G	*Was*, not <u>were</u>
2.	D	*Resented* for <u>admired</u>
3.	G	*Depends* for <u>depend</u>
4.	G	*Is* for <u>are</u>
5.	O	
6.	O	
7.	D	*Careful*, not <u>captious</u>
8.	V	Eliminate <u>completely and radically</u>
9.	G	*Had you studied...* is to be substituted for <u>If you would have studied</u>
10.	D	*Lucrative*, not <u>lucid</u>
11.	O	
12.	G	*Become*, not <u>becomes</u>
13.	G	Use *was* instead of <u>were</u>
14.	O	
15.	G	*Was destroyed*, not <u>were destroyed</u>
16.	O	
17.	G	*Who*, not <u>whom</u>
18.	G	*Who*, not <u>whom</u>
19.	O	
20.	G	Attain parallelism by placing <u>arose</u> at the end of this sentence

----

TEST 5

DIRECTIONS: Among the sentences in this test are some which cannot be accepted in formal, written English for one or another of the following reasons:

POOR DICTION: The use of a word which is improper either because its meaning does not fit the sentence or because it is not acceptable in formal writing.
Example: The audience was strongly effected by the senator's speech.

VERBOSITY: Repetitious elements adding nothing to the meaning of the sentence and not justified by any need for special emphasis.
Example: At that time there was then no right of petition.

FAULTY GRAMMAR: Word forms and expressions which do not conform to the grammatical and structural usages required by formal written English (errors in case, number, parallelism, and the like).
Example: Everyone in the delegation had their reasons for opposing the measure.

No sentence has more than one kind of error. Some sentences have no errors. Read each sentence carefully; then, in the space at the right, print the letter:
    D if the sentence contains an error in diction
    V if the sentence is verbose
    G if the sentence contains faulty grammar
    O if the sentence contains none of these errors

1.   The town consists of three distinct sections, of which the western one is by far the larger.   1.____

2.   Of London and Paris, the former is the wealthiest.   2.____

3.   The omniscient clap of thunder was not followed by a storm.   3.____

4.   Chicago is larger than any city in Illinois.   4.____

5.   America is the greatest nation, and of all other nations England is the greater.   5.____

6.   Amalgamating their forces helped the two generals to defeat the enemy.   6.____

7.   There are very good and sufficient grounds for such a decision.   7.____

8.   Due to bad weather, the game was postponed.   8.____

9.   The door opens, and in walks John and Mary.   9.____

10.   Where but America is there greater prosperity?   10.____

11.   The coffee grounds left a sedentary deposit in the cup.   11.____

12.   I can but do my best.   12.____

13.   I cannot help but comparing him with his predecessor.   13.____

14.   Many of Aesop's Fables are parodies from which we can profit.   14.____

15. I wish that I was in Florida now.   15.____

16. I like this kind of grapes better than any other.   16.____

17. The remainder of the time was spent in prayer.   17.____

18. Immigration is when people come into a foreign country to live.   18.____

19. He coughed continuously last winter.   19.____

20. The method is different than the one that was formerly used.   20.____

———

KEY (CORRECT ANSWERS)

1. G   *Largest* for <u>larger</u>
2. G   Wealthier for <u>wealthiest</u>
3. D   *Ominous*, not <u>omniscient</u>
4. G   Insert *other* before <u>city</u>
5. G   *Greatest* should replace <u>greater</u> at the end of this sentence
6. O
7. V   Eliminate <u>and sufficient</u>
8. G   *Because of*, not <u>due to</u>
9. G   *Walk*, not <u>walks</u>
10. G   Insert *in* before <u>America</u>
11. D   *Sedimentary*, not <u>sedentary</u>
12. O
13. G   Eliminate <u>but</u>
14. D   *Parables*, not <u>parodies</u>
15. G   *Were*, not <u>was</u>
16. O
17. O
18. G   Rewrite: *Immigration denotes people coming into...*
19. D   *Continually*, not <u>continuously</u>
20. G   *From*, not <u>than</u>

———

WRITTEN ENGLISH EXPRESSION
EXAMINATION SECTION
TEST 1

DIRECTIONS: In each of the following groups of sentences, one of the four sentences is faulty in grammar, punctuation, or capitalization. Select the incorrect sentence in each case. *PRINT THE LETTER OF THE CORRECT ANSWER IN THE SPACE AT THE RIGHT.*

1. A. If you had stood at home and done your homework, you would not have failed in arithmetic.
    B. Her affected manner annoyed every member of the audience.
    C. How will the new law affect our income taxes?
    D. The plants were not affected by the long, cold winter, but they succumbed to the drought of summer.

1.____

2. A. He is one of the most able men who have been in the Senate.
    B. It is he who is to blame for the lamentable mistake.
    C. Haven't you a helpful suggestion to make at this time?
    D. The money was robbed from the blind man's cup.

2.____

3. A. The amount of children in this school is steadily increasing.
    B. After taking an apple from the table, she went out to play.
    C. He borrowed a dollar from me.
    D. I had hoped my brother would arrive before me.

3.____

4. A. Whom do you think I hear from every week?
    B. Who do you think is the right man for the job?
    C. Who do you think I found in the room?
    D. He is the man whom we considered a good candidate for the presidency.

4.____

5. A. Quietly the puppy laid down before the fireplace.
    B. You have made your bed; now lie in it.
    C. I was badly sunburned because I had lain too long in the sun.
    D. I laid the doll on the bed and left the room.

5.____

6. A. Sailing down the bay was a thrilling experience for me.
    B. He was not consulted about your joining the club.
    C. This story is different than the one I told you yesterday.
    D. There is no doubt about his being the best player.

6.____

7. A. He maintains there is but one road to world peace.
    B. It is common knowledge that a child sees much he is not supposed to see.
    C. Much of the bitterness might have been avoided if arbitration had been restored to earlier in the meeting.
    D. The man decided it would be advisable to marry a girl somewhat younger than him.

7.____

8.
   A.   In this book, the incident I liked least is where the hero tries to put out the forest fire.

   B.   Learning a foreign language will undoubtedly give a person a better understanding of his mother tongue.

   C.   His actions made us wonder what he planned to do next.

   D.   Because of the war, we were unable to travel during the summer vacation.

8.____

9.
   A.   The class had no sooner become interested in the lesson than the dismissal bell rang.

   B.   There is little agreement about the kind of world to be planned at the peace conference.

   C.   "Today," said the teacher, "we shall read 'The Wind in the Willows.' I am sure you'll like it."

   D.   The terms of the legal settlement of the family quarrel handicapped both sides for many years.

9.____

10.
   A.   I was so surprised that I was not able to say a word.

   B.   She is taller than any other member of the class.

   C.   It would be much more preferable if you were never seen in his company.

   D.   We had no choice but to excuse her for being late.

10.____

———

KEY (CORRECT ANSWERS)

1.	A	6.	C
2.	D	7.	D
3.	A	8.	A
4.	C	9.	C
5.	A	10.	C

———

TEST 2

DIRECTIONS: In each of the following groups of sentences, one of the four sentences is faulty in grammar, punctuation, or capitalization. Select the incorrect sentence in each case. *PRINT THE LETTER OF THE CORRECT ANSWER IN THE SPACE AT THE RIGHT.*

1.   A.   Please send me these data at the earliest opportunity.   1.____
      B.   The loss of their material proved to be a severe handicap.
      C.   My principal objection to this plan is that it is impracticable.
      D.   The doll had laid in the rain for an hour and was ruined.

2.   A.   The garden scissors, left out all night in the rain, were in a badly rusted condition.   2.____
      B.   The girls felt bad about the misunderstanding which had arisen.
      C.   Sitting near the campfire, the old man told John and I about many exciting adventures he had had.
      D.   Neither of us is in a position to undertake a task of that magnitude.

3.   A.   The general concluded that one of the three roads would lead to the besieged city.   3.____
      B.   The children didn't, as a rule, do hardly anything beyond what they were told to do.
      C.   The reason the girl gave for her negligence was that she had acted on the spur of the moment.
      D.   The daffodils and tulips look beautiful in that blue vase.

4.   A.   If I was ten years older, I should be interested in this work.   4.____
      B.   Give the prize to whoever has drawn the best picture.
      C.   When you have finished reading the book, take it back to the library.
      D.   My drawing is as good as or better than yours.

5.   A.   He asked me whether the substance was animal or vegetable.   5.____
      B.   An apple which is unripe should not be eaten by a child.
      C.   That was an insult to me who am your friend.
      D.   Some spy must of reported the matter to the enemy.

6.   A.   Limited time makes quoting the entire message impossible.   6.____
      B.   Who did she say was going?
      C.   The girls in your class have dressed more dolls this year than we.
      D.   There was such a large amount of books on the floor that I couldn't find a place for my rocking chair.

7.   A.   What with his sleeplessness and his ill health, he was unable to assume any responsibility for the success of the meeting.   7.____
      B.   If I had been born in February, I should be celebrating my birthday soon.
      C.   In order to prevent breakage, she placed a sheet of paper between each of the plates when she packed them.
      D.   After the spring shower, the violets smelled very sweet.

8.   A.   He had laid the book down very reluctantly before the end of the lesson.   8.____
      B.   The dog, I am sorry to say, had lain on the bed all night.
      C.   The cloth was first lain on a flat surface; then it was pressed with a hot iron.
      D.   While we were in Florida, we lay in the sun until we were noticeably tanned.

9.   A.   If John was in New York during the recent holiday season, I have no doubt he spent   9.____
            most of his time with his parents.
    B.   How could he enjoy the television program; the dog was barking and the baby
            was crying.
    C.   When the problem was explained to the class, he must have been asleep.
    D.   She wished that her new dress were finished so that she could go to the party.

10.   A.   The engine not only furnishes power but light and heat as well.   10.____
     B.   You're aware that we've forgotten whose guilt was established, aren't you?
     C.   Everybody knows that the woman made many sacrifices for her children.
     D.   A man with his dog and gun is a familiar sight in this neighborhood.

KEY (CORRECT ANSWERS)

1.	D		6.	D
2.	C		7.	B
3.	B		8.	C
4.	A		9.	B
5.	D		10.	A

TEST 3

DIRECTIONS: Each of sentences 1 to 18 may be classified most appropriately under one of the following three categories:
- A. faulty because of incorrect grammar
- B. faulty because of incorrect punctuation
- C. correct

Examine each sentence carefully. Then, in the space at the right, print the capital letter preceding the option which is best of the three suggested above. All incorrect sentences contain but one type of error. Consider a sentence correct if it contains none of the types of errors mentioned, even though there may be other correct ways of expressing the same thought.

1. He sent the notice to the clerk who you hired yesterday.   1._____

2. It must be admitted, however that you were not informed of this change.   2._____

3. Only the employees who have served in this grade for at least two years are eligible for promotion.   3._____

4. The work was divided equally between she and Mary.   4._____

5. He thought that you were not available at that time.   5._____

6. When the messenger returns; please give him this package.   6._____

7. The new secretary prepared, typed, addressed, and delivered, the notices.   7._____

8. Walking into the room, his desk can be seen at the rear.   8._____

9. Although John has worked here longer than she, he produces a smaller amount of work.   9._____

10. She said she could of typed this report yesterday.   10._____

11. Neither one of these procedures are adequate for the efficient performance of this task.   11._____

12. The typewriter is the tool of the typist; the cash register, the tool of the cashier.   12._____

13. "The assignment must be completed as soon as possible" said the supervisor.   13._____

14. As you know, office handbooks are issued to all new employees.   14._____

15. Writing a speech is sometimes easier than to deliver it before an audience.   15._____

16. Mr. Brown our accountant, will audit the accounts next week.   16._____

17. Give the assignment to whomever is able to do it most efficiently.   17._____

18. The supervisor expected either your or I to file these reports.   18._____

KEY (CORRECT ANSWERS)

1. A	6. B	11. A	16. B
2. B	7. B	12. C	17. A
3. C	8. A	13. B	18. A
4. A	9. C	14. C	
5. C	10. A	15. A	

———

TEST 4

DIRECTIONS: Each sentence may be classified most appropriately under one of the following four categories:
  A. faulty because of incorrect grammar
  B. faulty because of incorrect punctuation
  C. faulty because of incorrect spelling
  D. correct

Examine each sentence carefully. Then, in the space at the right, write the capital letter preceding the best of the four alternatives suggested above. All incorrect sentences contain but one type of error. Consider a sentence correct if it contains none of the types of errors mentioned, even though there may be other correct ways of expressing the same thought.

1. The fire apparently started in the storeroom, which is usually locked.   1.____

2. On approaching the victim two bruises were noticed by this officer.   2.____

3. The officer, who was there examined the report with great care.   3.____

4. Each employee in the office had a seperate desk.   4.____

5. All employees including members of the clerical staff, were invited to the lecture.   5.____

6. The suggested procedure is similar to the one now in use.   6.____

7. No one was more pleased with the new procedure than the chauffeur.   7.____

8. He tried to pursuade her to change the procedure.   8.____

9. The total of the expenses charged to petty cash were high.   9.____

10. An understanding between him and I was finally reached.   10.____

KEY (CORRECT ANSWERS)

1.	D		6.	D
2.	A		7.	D
3.	B		8.	C
4.	C		9.	A
5.	B		10.	A

TEST 5

Questions 1-5.

DIRECTIONS: Each of sentences 1 to 5 may be classified under one of the following four categories:
    A. faulty because of incorrect grammar
    B. faulty because of incorrect punctuation
    C. faulty because of incorrect capitalization or incorrect spelling
    D. correct
Examine each sentence carefully to determined under which of the above four options it is best classified. Then, in the space at the right, print the capital letter preceding the option which is the best of the four suggested above. Each faulty sentence contains but one type of error. Consider a sentence to be correct if it contains none of the types of errors mentioned, even though there may be other correct ways of expressing the same thought.

1. They told both he and I that the prisoner had escaped.   1._____

2. Any superior officer, who, disregards the just complaints of his subordinates, is remiss in the performance of his duty.   2._____

3. Only those members of the national organization who resided in the Middle West attended the conference in Chicago.   3._____

4. We told him to give the investigation assignment to whoever was available.   4._____

5. Please do not disappoint and embarass us by not appearing in court.   5._____

Questions 6-10.

DIRECTIONS: Each of questions 6 to 10 consists of a sentence. Read each sentence carefully and then write your answer to each question according to the following scheme:
    A. sentence contains an error in spelling only
    B. sentence contains an error in grammar or word usage only
    C. sentence contains one error in spelling and one error in grammar or word usage
    D. sentence is correct; contains no errors

6. Although the officer's speech proved to be entertaining, the topic was not relevant to the main theme of the conference.   6._____

7. In Febuary all new officers attended a training course in which they were learned their principal duties and the fundamental operating procedures of the department.   7._____

8. I personally seen inmate Jones threaten inmates Smith and Green with bodily harm if they refused to participate in the plot.   8._____

9. To the layman, who on a chance visit to the prison observes everything functioning smoothly, the maintenance of prison discipline may seem to be a relatively easily realizable objective.   9._____

10. The prisoners in cell block fourty were forbidden to lay on the cell cots during the recre-   10.____
    ation hour.

———

KEY (CORRECT ANSWERS)

1.	A	6.	D
2.	B	7.	C
3.	C	8.	B
4.	D	9.	D
5.	C	10.	C

———

TEST 6

DIRECTIONS: Each of the following sentences may be classified under one of the following four categories:

    A. faulty because of incorrect grammar
    B. faulty because of incorrect punctuation
    C. faulty because of incorrect capitalization or incorrect spelling
    D. correct

Examine each sentence carefully to determine under which of the above four options it is best classified. Then, in the space at the right, print the capital letter preceding the option which is the best of the four suggested above. Each faulty sentence contains but one type of error. Consider a sentence to be correct if it contains none of the types of errors mentioned, even though there may be other correct ways of expressing the same thought.

1.   I cannot encourage you any.   1._____

2.   You always look well in those sort of clothes.   2._____

3.   Shall we go to the park?   3._____

4.   The man whome he introduced was Mr. Carey.   4._____

5.   She saw the letter laying here this morning.   5._____

6.   It should rain before the Afternoon is over.   6._____

7.   They have already went home.   7._____

8.   That Jackson will be elected is evident.   8._____

9.   He does not hardly approve of us.   9._____

10.   It was he, who won the prize.   10._____

KEY (CORRECT ANSWERS)

1.	A	6.	C
2.	A	7.	A
3.	D	8.	D
4.	C	9.	A
5.	A	10.	B

TEST 7

DIRECTIONS: Each of the following sentences may be classified under one of the following four categories:
  A. faulty because of incorrect grammar
  B. faulty because of incorrect punctuation
  C. faulty because of incorrect capitalization or incorrect spelling
  D. correct

Examine each sentence carefully to determine under which of the above four options is best classified. Then, in the space at the right, print the capital letter preceding the option which is the best of the four suggested above. Each faulty sentence contains but one type of error. Consider a sentence to be correct if it contains none of the types of errors mentioned, even though there may be other correct ways of expressing the same thought.

1. Shall we go to the park.   1._____

2. They are, alike, in this particular.   2._____

3. They gave the poor man sume food when he knocked on the door.   3._____

4. I regret the loss caused by the error.   4._____

5. The students' will have a new teacher.   5._____

6. They sweared to bring out all the facts.   6._____

7. He decided to open a branch store on 33rd street.   7._____

8. His speed is equal and more than that of a racehorse.   8._____

9. He felt very warm on that Summer day.   9._____

10. He was assisted by his friend, who lives in the next house.   10._____

KEY (CORRECT ANSWERS)

1.	B	6.	A
2.	B	7.	C
3.	C	8.	A
4.	D	9.	C
5.	B	10.	D

TEST 8

DIRECTIONS: Each of the following sentences may be classified under one of the following four categories:

    A.   faulty because of incorrect grammar
    B.   faulty because of incorrect punctuation
    C.   faulty because of incorrect capitalization or incorrect spelling
    D.   correct

Examine each sentence carefully to determine under which of the above four options it is best classified. Then, in the space at the right, print the capital letter preceding the option which is the best of the four suggested above. Each faulty sentence contains but one type of error. Consider a sentence to be correct if it contains none of the types of errors mentioned, even though there may be other correct ways of expressing the same thought.

1. The climate of New York is colder than California.   1.____

2. I shall wait for you on the corner.   2.____

3. Did we see the boy who, we think, is the leader.   3.____

4. Being a modest person, John seldom talks about his invention.   4.____

5. The gang is called the smith street boys.   5.____

6. He seen the man break into the store.   6.____

7. We expected to lay still there for quite a while.   7.____

8. He is considered to be the Leader of his organization.   8.____

9. Although I recieved an invitation, I won't go.   9.____

10. The letter must be here some place.   10.____

KEY (CORRECT ANSWERS)

1.	A	6.	A
2.	D	7.	A
3.	B	8.	C
4.	D	9.	C
5.	C	10.	A

TEST 9

DIRECTIONS: Each of the following sentences may be classified under one of the following four categories:
  A. faulty because of incorrect grammar
  B. faulty because of incorrect punctuation
  C. faulty because of incorrect capitalization or incorrect spelling
  D. correct

Examine each sentence carefully to determine under which of the above four options it is best classified. Then, in the space at the right, print the capital letter preceding the option which is the best of the four suggested above. Each faulty sentence contains but one type of error. Consider a sentence to be correct if it contains none of the types of errors mentioned, even though there may be other correct ways of expressing the same thought.

1. I thought it to be he.   1.____

2. We expect to remain here for a long time.   2.____

3. The committee was agreed.   3.____

4. Two-thirds of the building are finished.   4.____

5. The water was froze.   5.____

6. Everyone of the salesmen must supply their own car.   6.____

7. Who is the author of Gone With The Wind?   7.____

8. He marched on and declaring that he would never surrender.   8.____

9. Who shall I say called?   9.____

10. Everyone has left but they.   10.____

KEY (CORRECT ANSWERS)

1.	A	6.	A
2.	D	7.	B
3.	A	8.	A
4.	A	9.	D
5.	A	10.	D

TEST 10

DIRECTIONS: Each of the following sentences may be classified under one of the following four categories:
   A. faulty because of incorrect grammar
   B. faulty because of incorrect punctuation
   C. faulty because of incorrect capitalization or incorrect spelling
   D. correct

Examine each sentence carefully to determine under which of the above four options it is best classified. Then, in the space at the right, print the capital letter preceding the option which is the best of the four suggested above. Each faulty sentence contains but one type of error. Consider a sentence to be correct if it contains none of the types of errors mentioned, even though there may be other correct ways of expressing the same thought.

1. Who did we give the order to?   1.____

2. Send your order in immediately.   2.____

3. I believe I paid the Bill.   3.____

4. I have not met but one person.   4.____

5. Why aren't Tom, and Fred, going to the dance?   5.____

6. What reason is there for him not going?   6.____

7. The seige of Malta was a tremendous event.   7.____

8. I was there yesterday I assure you.   8.____

9. Your ukelele is better than mine.   9.____

10. No one was there only Mary.   10.____

KEY (CORRECT ANSWERS)

1.	A		6.	A
2.	D		7.	C
3.	C		8.	B
4.	A		9.	C
5.	B		10.	A

EXAMINATION SECTION
TEST 1

DIRECTIONS: Each question or incomplete statement is followed by several suggested answers or completions. Select the one that BEST answers the question or completes the statement. *PRINT THE LETTER OF THE CORRECT ANSWER IN THE SPACE AT THE RIGHT.*

Questions 1-25.

A student has written an article for the high school newspaper, using the skills learned in a stenography and typewriting class in its preparation. In the article which follows, certain words or groups of words are underlined and numbered. The underlined word or group of words may be incorrect because they present an error in grammar, usage, sentence structure, capitalization, diction, or punctuation. For each numbered word or group of words, there is an identically numbered question consisting of four choices based only on the underlined portion. Indicate the BEST choice. Unnecessary changes will be considered incorrect.

TIGERS VIE FOR CITY CHAMPIONSHIP

In their second year of varsity football, the North Side Tigers have gained a shot at the city championship. Last Saturday in the play-offs, the Tigers defeated the Western High
(1)
School Cowboys, thus eliminated that team from contention. Most of the credit for the
(2)
team's improvement must go to Joe Harris, the coach. To play as well as they do now, the coach
(3)
must have given the team superior instruction. There is no doubt that, if a coach is effective, his
influence is over many young minds.
(4)

With this major victory behind them, the Tigers can now look forward to meet the defending champions, the Revere Minutemen, in the finals.

(5)
The win over the Cowboys was due to North Side's supremacy in the air. The Tigers'
(6)
players have the advantages of strength and of being speedy. Our sterling quarterback, Butch
(7)
Carter, a master of the long pass, used these kind of passes to bedevil the boys from
(8)
Western. As a matter of fact, if the Tigers would have used the passing offense earlier in the game, the score would have been more one-sided. Butch, by the way, our all-around senior student, has already been tapped for bigger things. Having the highest marks in his class, Barton
(9)
College has offered him a scholarship.

The team's defense is another story. During the last few weeks, neither the linebackers

(10)

nor the safety man <u>have shown</u> sufficient ability to contain their oppo nents' running game.

(11)

In the city final, <u>the defensive unit's failing to complete it's assignments</u> may lead to disaster.

(12)

However, the coach said that this unit <u>not only has been cooperative but also the coach raise</u>

(13)

<u>their eagerness to learn</u>. He also said that this team <u>has</u> not <u>and never will give up</u>.

(14)

This kind of spirit is contagious, <u>therefore</u> I predict that the Tigers will   win because I have

(15)

<u>affection and full confidence in</u> the team.

(16)

One of the happy surprises this season is Peter Yisko, our punter. Peter <u>is</u> in the United

States for only two years. When he was in grammar school in the old country, it was not nec-

(17)

essary for him <u>to have studied</u> hard. Now, he depends on the football team to help him with

(18)

his English. Everybody <u>but the team mascot and I have</u> been pressed into service. Peter was

(19)

ineligible last year when he <u>learned that he would only obtain half</u> of the credits he had com-

pleted in Europe. Nevertheless, he attended occasional practice sessions, but he soon found

(20)

out that, if one wants to be a success ful player, <u>you</u> must realize that regular practice is

(21)

required. In fact, if a team is to be successful, it is necessary that everyone <u>be</u> present for all

(22)

practice sessions. "The life of a football player," says Peter, "is better than <u>a scholar</u>."

Facing the Minutemen, the Tigers will meet their most formidable opposition yet. This

(23)

team <u>is not only gaining a bad reputation</u> but also indulging in illegal practices on the field.

(24)

They <u>can't hardly object to us being</u> technical about penalties under these circumstances.

(25)

As far as the Minutemen are concerned, a <u>victory will taste sweet like a victory should</u>.

1. A. that eliminated that team
    B. and they were eliminated
    C. and eliminated them
    D. Correct as is

1.____

2. A. To make them play as well as they do
    B. Having played so well
    C. After they played so well
    D. Correct as is

2.____

3. A. if coaches are effective; they have influence over
    B. to be effective, a coach influences
    C. if a coach is effective, he influences
    D. Correct as is

3.____

4.	A. to meet with	B. to meeting	4._____	
	C. to a meeting of	D. Correct as is		

5.	A. because of	B. on account of	5._____	
	C. motivated by	D. Correct as is		

6.	A. operating swiftly	B. speed	6._____	
	C. running speedily	D. Correct as is		

7.	A. these kinds of pass	B. this kind of passes	7._____	
	C. this kind of pass	D. Correct as is		

8.	A. would of used	B. had used	8._____	
	C. were using	D. Correct as is		

9. 9._____
A. he was offered a scholarship by Barton College.
B. Barton College offered a scholarship to him.
C. a scholarship was offered him by Barton College.
D. Correct as is

10.	A. had shown	B. were showing	10._____	
	C. has shown	D. Correct as is		

11. 11._____
A. the defensive unit failing to complete its assignment
B. the defensive unit's failing to complete its assignment
C. the defensive unit failing to complete it's assignment
D. Correct as is

12. 12._____
A. has been not only cooperative, but also eager to learn
B. has not only been cooperative, but also shows eagerness to learn
C. has been not only cooperative, but also they were eager to learn
D. Correct as is

13. 13._____
A. has not given up and never will
B. has not and never would give up
C. has not given up and never will give up
D. Correct as is

14.	A. . Therefore	B. : therefore	14._____	
	C. -- therefore	D. Correct as is		

15. 15._____
A. full confidence and affection for
B. affection for and full confidence in
C. affection and full confidence concerning
D. Correct as is

16.	A. is living	B. was living	16._____	
	C. has been	D. Correct as is		

17.	A. to study	B. to be studying	17._____	
	C. to have been studying	D. Correct as is		

18. A. but the team mascot and me has
     B. but the team mascot and myself has
     C. but the team mascot and me have
     D. Correct as is

18.____

19. A. only learned that he would obtain half
     B. learned that he would obtain only half
     C. learned that he only would obtain half
     D. Correct as is

19.____

20. A. a person   B. everyone
     C. one   D. one

20.____

21. A. is   B. will be
     C. shall be   D. Correct as is

21.____

22. A. to be a scholar   B. being a scholar
     C. that of a scholar   D. Correct as is

22.____

23. A. not only is gaining a bad reputation
     B. is gaining not only a bad reputation
     C. is not gaining only a bad reputation
     D. Correct as is

23.____

24. A. can hardly object to us being
     B. can hardly object to our being
     C. can't hardly object to our being
     D. Correct as is

24.____

25. A. victory will taste sweet like it should
     B. victory will taste sweetly as it should taste
     C. victory will taste sweet as a victory should
     D. Correct as is

25.____

Questions 26-30.

DIRECTIONS: Questions 26 through 30 are to be answered on the basis of the instructions and paragraph which follow.

The paragraph which follows is part of a report prepared by a buyer for submission to his superior. The paragraph contains 5 underlined groups of words, each one bearing a number which identifies the question relating to it. Each of these groups of words MAY or MAY NOT represent standard written English, suitable for use in a formal report. For each question, decide whether the group of words used in the paragraph which is always choice A is standard written English and should be retained, or whether choice B, C, or D.

On October 23, 2009 the vendor delivered two microscopes to the using agency. When (26) they inspected, one microscope was found to have a defective part. The vendor was notified,

and offered to replace the defective part; the using agency, however, requested that the (27) microscope be replaced. The vendor claimed that complete replacement was unnecessary and

(28)

refused to comply with the agency's demand, <u>having the result that the agency declared</u> that it

(29)

will pay only for the acceptable microscope. At that point <u>I got involved by the agency's</u>

<u>contacting me</u>. The agency requested that I speak to the vendor since I handled the original

(30)

purchase and <u>have dealt with this vendor before</u>.

26.   A.   When they inspected,   26.____
           B.   Upon inspection,
           C.   The inspection report said that
           D.   Having inspected,

27.   A.   that the microscope be replaced.   27.____
           B.   a whole new microscope in replacement.
           C.   to have a replacement for the microscope.
           D.   that they get the microscope replaced.

28.   A.   , having the result that the agency declared   28.____
           B.   ; the agency consequently declared
           C.   , which refusal caused the agency to consequently declare
           D.   , with the result of the agency's declaring

29.   A.   I got involved by the agency's contacting me.   29.____
           B.   I became involved, being contacted by the agency.
           C.   the agency contacting me, I got involved.
           D.   the agency contacted me and I became involved.

30.   A.   have dealt with this vendor before.   30.____
           B.   done business before with this vendor.
           C.   know this vendor by prior dealings.
           D.   have dealt with this vendor before.

KEY (CORRECT ANSWERS)

1.	C		16.	C
2.	A		17.	A
3.	C		18.	A
4.	B		19.	B
5.	A		20.	C
6.	B		21.	D
7.	C		22.	C
8.	B		23.	D
9.	D		24.	A
10.	C		25.	C
11.	B		26.	B
12.	A		27.	A
13.	B		28.	B
14.	A		29.	D
15.	B		30.	D

ENGLISH GRAMMAR and USAGE

EXAMINATION SECTION
TEST 1

DIRECTIONS: In the passages that follow, certain words and phrases are underlined and numbered. In each question, you will find alternatives for each underlined part. You are to choose the one that BEST expresses the idea, makes the statement appropriate for standard written English, or is worded MOST consistently with the style and tone of the passage as a whole. Choose the alternative you consider BEST and write the letter in the space at the right. If you think the original version is BEST, choose NO CHANGE. Read each passage through once before you begin to answer the questions that accompany it. You cannot determine most answers without reading several sentences beyond the phrase in question. Be sure that you have read far enough ahead each time you choose an alternative.

Questions 1-14.

DIRECTIONS: Questions 1 through 14 are based on the following passage.

Modern filmmaking <u>hadbegan</u> in Paris in 1895 with the work of the Lumiere brothers.
                          1

Using their <u>invention, the Cinématographe</u> the Lumières were able to photograph, print,
                          2

and project moving pictures onto a screen. Their films showed <u>actual occurrences.</u> <u>A</u> train
                                                                                    3

approaching a station, people leaving a factory, workers demolishing a wall.

These early films had neither plot nor sound. But another Frenchman, Georges Méliès,

soon incorporated plot lines <u>into</u> his films. And with his attempts to draw upon the potential of
                                4

film to create fantasy <u>worlds.</u> Méliès also <u>was an early pioneer from</u> special film effects.
                          5   6

Edwin S. Porter, an American filmmaker, took Méliès's emphasis on narrative one step further.

Believing <u>that, continuity of shots</u> was of primary importance in filmmaking, Porter connected
              7

<u>images to present,</u> a sustained action. His GREAT TRAIN ROBBERY of 1903 opened a new
        8

era in film.

<u>Because</u> film was still considered <u>as</u> low entertainment in early twentieth century Amer-
    9   10

ica, it was on its way to becoming a respected art form. Beginning in 1908, the American director D.W. Griffith discovered and explored techniques to make film a more expressive

medium. With his technical contributions, $\underline{\text{as well as}}$ his attempts to develop the intellec-
11

tual and moral potential of film, Griffith helped build a solid foundation for the industry.

$\underline{\text{Thirty}}$ years after the Lumière brothers' first show, sound $\underline{\text{had yet been}}$ added to the
12 13

movies. Finally, in 1927, Hollywood pro duced its first *talkie,* THE JAZZ SINGER. With sound,

modern film $\underline{\text{coming}}$ of age.
14

1. A. NO CHANGE
   B. begun
   C. began
   D. had some beginnings

1.____

2. A. NO CHANGE
   B. hinvention - the Cinématogrape
   C. invention, the Cinématographe -
   D. invention, the Cinématographe

2.____

3. A. NO CHANGE
   B. actually occurrences, a
   C. actually occurrences - a
   D. actual occurrences: a

3.____

4. A. NO CHANGE
   B. about
   C. with
   D. to

4.____

5. A. NO CHANGE
   B. worlds,
   C. worlds; and
   D. worlds and

5.____

6. A. NO CHANGE
   B. pioneered
   C. pioneered the beginnings of
   D. pioneered the early beginnings of

6.____

7. A. NO CHANGE
   B. that continuity of shots
   C. that, continuity of shots,
   D. that continuity of shots

7.____

8. A. NO CHANGE
   B. images to present
   C. images and present
   D. images, and presenting

8.____

9. A. NO CHANGE
    B. (Begin new paragraph) In view of the fact that
    C. (Begin new paragraph) Although
    D. (Do NOT begin new paragraph) Since

9.____

10. A. NO CHANGE
    B. as if it were
    C. like it was
    D. OMIT the underlined portion

10.____

11. A. NO CHANGE
    B. similar to
    C. similar with
    D. like with

11.____

12. A. NO CHANGE
    B. (Begin new paragraph) Consequently, thirty
    C. (Do NOT begin new paragraph) Therefore, thirty
    D. (Do NOT begin new paragraph) As a consequence, thirty

12.____

13. A. NO CHANGE
    B. had yet to be
    C. has yet
    D. was yet being

13.____

14. A. NO CHANGE
    B. comes
    C. came
    D. had came

14.____

Questions 15-22.

DIRECTIONS: Questions 15 through 22 are based on the following passage.

One of the most awesome forces in nature is the tsunami, or tidal wave. A
tsunami - the word is Japanese for harbor wave, can generate the destructive power of many
                          15
atomic bombs.

Tsunamis usually appear in a series of four or five waves about fifteen minutes apart.
        16
They begin deep in the ocean, gather remarkable speed as they travel, and cover great dis-
tances. The wave triggered by the explosion of Krakatoa in 1883 circled the world in three days.

Tsunamis being known to sink large ships at sea, they are most dangerous when they
        17
reach land. Close to shore, an oncoming tsunami is forced upward and skyward, perhaps
                                                                          18
as high as 100 feet. This combination of height and speed accounts for the tsunami's

great power.

That *tsunami* is a Japanese word is no accident, <u>due to the fact that</u> no nation
$\qquad\qquad\qquad\qquad\qquad\qquad\qquad\quad$ 19

<u>frequently</u> has been so visited by giant waves as Japan. <u>Tsunamis</u> reach that country regu-
20 $\qquad\qquad\qquad\qquad\qquad\qquad\qquad\qquad\qquad\qquad$ 21

larly, and with devastating consequences. One Japanese tsunami flattened several towns in

<u>1896, also killed 27,000 people.</u> The 2011 tsunami caused similar loss of life as well as
$\qquad\qquad$ 22

untold damage from nuclear radiation.

15. A. NO CHANGE
    B. tsunami, the word is Japanese for harbor wave -
    C. tsunami - the word is Japanese for harbor wave -
    D. tsunami - the word being Japanese for harbor wave,

15.____

16. A. NO CHANGE
    B. (Begin new paragraph) Consequently, tsunamis
    C. (Do NOT begin new paragraph) Tsunamis consequently
    D. (Do NOT begin new paragraph) Yet, tsunamis

16.____

17. A. NO CHANGE
    B. Because tsunamis have been
    C. Although tsunamis have been
    D. Tsunamis have been

17.____

18. A. NO CHANGE
    B. upward to the sky,
    C. upward in the sky,
    D. upward,

18.____

19. A. NO CHANGE
    B. when one takes into consideration the fact that
    C. seeing as how
    D. for

19.____

20. A. NO CHANGE
    B. (Place after *has*)
    C. (Place after *so*)
    D. (Place after *visited*)

20.____

21. A. NO CHANGE
    B. Moreover, tsunamis
    C. However, tsunamis
    D. Because tsunamis

21.____

22. A. NO CHANGE
    B. 1896 and killed 27,000 people.
    C. 1896 and killing 27,000 people.
    D. 1896, and 27,000 people as well.

22.____

Questions 23-33.

DIRECTIONS: Questions 23 through 33 are based on the following passage.

I was <u>married one</u> August on a farm in Maine. The <u>ceremony, itself, taking</u> place in an
       23   24

arbor of pine boughs <u>we had built and constructed</u> in the yard next to the house. On the
                             25

morning of the wedding day, we parked the tractors behind the shed, <u>have tied</u> the dogs to an
                                                               26

oak tree to keep them from chasing the guests, and put the cows out to pasture. <u>Thus</u> we had
                                                                           27

thought of everything, it seemed. we had forgotten how interested a cow can be in what is going

on <u>around them.</u> During the ceremony, my sister <u>(who has taken several years of lessons)</u>
       28   29

was to play a flute solo. We were all listening intently when she <u>had began</u> to play. As the first
                                                                        30

notes reached us, we were surprised to hear a bass line under the flute's treble melody. Looking

around, <u>the source was quicly discovered</u> . There was Star, my pet Guernsey, her head hang-
                                    31

ing over the pasture fence, mooing along with the delicate strains of Bach.

Star took our laughter <u>as being like</u> a compliment, and we took her contribution that way,
                                    32

too. <u>It was</u> a sign of approval - the kind you would find only at a farm wedding.
       33

23.   A.   NO CHANGE   23._____
        B.   married, one
        C.   married on an
        D.   married, in an

24.   A.   NO CHANGE   24._____
        B.   ceremony itself taking
        C.   ceremony itself took
        D.   ceremony, itself took

25.   A.   NO CHANGE   25._____
        B.   which had been built and constructed
        C.   we had built and constructed it
        D.   we had built

26.   A.   NO CHANGE   26._____
        B.   tie
        C.   tied
        D.   tying

27.   A.   NO CHANGE   27._____
        B.   (Do NOT begin new paragraph) And
        C.   (Begin new paragraph) But
        D.   (Begin new paragraph) Moreover,

28. A. NO CHANGE
    B. around her.
    C. in her own vicinity.
    D. in their immediate area.

    28.____

29. A. NO CHANGE
    B. (whom has taken many years of lessons)
    C. (who has been trained in music)
    D. OMIT the underlined portion

    29.____

30. A. NO CHANGE
    B. begun
    C. began
    D. would begin

    30.____

31. A. NO CHANGE
    B. the discovery of the source was quick.
    C. the discovery of the source was quickly made.
    D. we quickly discovered the source.

    31.____

32. A. NO CHANGE
    B. as
    C. just as
    D. as if

    32.____

33. A. NO CHANGE
    B. Yet it was
    C. But it was
    D. Being

    33.____

Questions 34-42.

DIRECTIONS: Questions 34 through 42 are based on the following passage.

Riding a bicycle in Great Britain is not the same as riding a bicycle in the United States. Americans bicycling in Britain will find some $\underset{34}{\underline{\text{basic fundamental}}}$ differences in the rules of the road and in the attitudes of motorists.

$\underset{35}{\underline{\text{Probably}}}$ most difficult for the American cyclist is adjusting $\underset{36}{\underline{\text{with}}}$ British traffic patterns. $\underset{37}{\underline{\text{Knowing that traffic}}}$ in Britain moves on the left-hand side of the road, bicycling $\underset{38}{\underline{\text{once}}}$ there is the mirror image of what it is in the United States.

The problem of adjusting to traffic patterns is somewhat lessened, $\underset{39}{\underline{\text{however}}}$ by the respect with which British motorists treat bicyclists. A cyclist in a traffic circle, for example, is given the same right-of-way $\underset{40}{\underline{\text{with}}}$ the driver of any other vehicle. However, the cyclist is expected to obey

the rules of the road. This <u>difference in the American and British attitudes toward bicyclists</u>
                                                              41

may stem from differing attitudes toward the bicycle itself. Whereas Americans frequently view

bicycles as <u>toys, but</u> the British treat them primarily as vehicles.
                  42

34. A. NO CHANGE   34.____
     B. basic and fundamental
     C. basically fundamental
     D. basic

35. A. NO CHANGE   35.____
     B. Even so, probably
     C. Therefore, probably
     D. As a result, probably

36. A. NO CHANGE   36.____
     B. upon
     C. on
     D. to

37. A. NO CHANGE   37.____
     B. Seeing that traffic
     C. Because traffic
     D. Traffic

38. A. NO CHANGE   38.____
     B. once you are
     C. once one is
     D. OMIT the underlined portion

39. A. NO CHANGE   39.____
     B. also,
     C. moreover,
     D. therefore,

40. A. NO CHANGE   40.____
     B. as
     C. as if
     D. as with

41. A. NO CHANGE   41.____
     B. difference in the American and British attitudes toward bicyclists
     C. difference, in the American and British attitudes toward bicyclists
     D. difference in the American, and British, attitudes toward bicyclists

42. A. NO CHANGE   42.____
     B. toys;
     C. toys,
     D. toys; but

Questions 43-51.

DIRECTIONS: Questions 43 through 51 are based on the following passage.

People have always believed that supernatural powers <u>tend toward some influence on</u>
43

lives for good or for ill. Superstition originated with the idea that individuals <u>could in turn,</u> exert
44

influence <u>at</u> spirits. Certain superstitions are <u>so deeply embedded</u> in our culture that intelli-
45   46

gent people sometimes act in accordance with them.

One common superstitious act is knocking on wood after boasting of good fortune. People once believed that gods inhabited trees and, therefore, were present in the wood used to build houses. Fearing that speaking of good luck within the gods' hearing might anger

<u>them, people</u> knocked on wood to deafen the gods and avoid their displeasure.
47

Another superstitious <u>custom and practice</u> is throwing salt over the left shoulder.
48

<u>Considering</u> salt was once considered sacred, people thought that spilling it brought bad luck.
49

Since right and left represented good and evil, the believers used their right hands, which sym-
bolized good, to throw a pinch of salt over their left shoulders into the eyes of the evil gods.

<u>Because of this,</u> people attempted to avert misfortune.
50

Without realizing the origin of superstitions, many people exhibit superstitious behavior.

<u>Others avoid</u> walking under ladders and stepping on cracks in sidewalks, without having any
51

idea why they are doing so.

43.   A.   NO CHANGE   43.___
      B.   can influence
      C.   tend to influence on
      D.   are having some influence on

44.   A.   NO CHANGE   44.___
      B.   could, turning,
      C.   could, in turn,
      D.   could, in turn

45.   A.   NO CHANGE   45.___
      B.   of
      C.   toward
      D.   on

46. A. NO CHANGE   46._____
     B. so deep embedded
     C. deepest embedded
     D. embedded deepest

47. A. NO CHANGE   47._____
     B. them; people
     C. them: some people
     D. them, they

48. A. NO CHANGE   48._____
     B. custom
     C. traditional custom
     D. customary habit

49. A. NO CHANGE   49._____
     B. Although
     C. Because
     D. Keeping in mind that

50. A. NO CHANGE   50._____
     B. As a result of this,
     C. Consequently,
     D. In this way,

51. A. NO CHANGE   51._____
     B. Often avoiding
     C. Avoiding
     D. They avoid

Questions 52-66.

DIRECTIONS: Questions 52 through 66 are based on the following passage.

In the 1920s, the Y.M.C.A. sponsored one of the first programs $\frac{\text{in order to promote}}{52}$ more

enlightened public opinion on racial matters; the organization started special university classes

$\frac{\text{in which}}{53}$ young people could study race relations. Among the guest speakers invited to conduct

the sessions, one of the most popular was George Washington Carver, the scientist from Tuske-
gee Institute.

As a student, Carver himself had been active in the Y.M.C.A. $\frac{\text{He shared}}{54}$ its evangelical

and educational philosophy. However, in $\frac{1923,}{55}$ the Y.M.C.A. arranged $\frac{\text{Carver's first initial}}{56}$

speaking tour, the scientist accepted with apprehension. He was to speak at several white col-
leges, most of whose students had never seen, let alone heard, an educated black man.

Although Carver's appearances <u>did sometimes</u> cause occasional <u>controversy, but</u> his
                                       57   58

quiet dedication prevailed, and his humor quickly won over his audiences. <u>Nevertheless, for</u>
                                                                                59

the next decade, Carver toured the Northeast, Midwest, and South under Y.M.C.A.

<u>sponsorship. Speaking</u> at places never before open to blacks. On these tours Carver
         60

befriended thousands of students, many of <u>whom</u> subsequently corresponded with
                                             61

his <u>afterwards.</u> The <u>tours, unfortunately were</u> not without discomfort for Carver. There were
       62   63

the indignities of *Jim Crow* accommodations and racial insults from strangers. <u>As a result,</u> the
                                                                                  64

scientist's enthusiasm never faltered. <u>Avoiding any discussion of</u> the political and social
                                                    65

aspects of racial injustice; instead, Carver conducted his whole life as an indirect attack <u>to</u>
                                                                                             66

prejudice. This, as much as his science, is his legacy to humankind.

52. A. NO CHANGE   52._____
    B. to promote
    C. for the promoting of what is
    D. for the promotion of what are

53. A. NO CHANGE   53._____
    B. from which
    C. that
    D. by which

54. A. No Change   54._____
    B. Sharing
    C. Having Shared
    D. Because He Shared

55. A. NO CHANGE   55._____
    B. 1923
    C. 1923, and
    D. 1923, when

56. A. NO CHANGE   56._____
    B. Carvers' first, initial
    C. Carvers first initial
    D. Carver's first

57. A. NO CHANGE
    B. sometimes did
    C. did
    D. OMIT the underlined portion

57.____

58. A. NO CHANGE
    B. controversy and
    C. controversy,
    D. controversy, however

58.____

59. A. NO CHANGE
    B. However, for
    C. However, from
    D. For

59.____

60. A. NO CHANGE
    B. sponsorship and spoke
    C. sponsorship; and spoke
    D. sponsorship, and speaking

60.____

61. A. NO CHANGE
    B. who
    C. them
    D. those

61.____

62. A. NO CHANGE
    B. later.
    C. sometime later.
    D. OMIT the underlined portion and end the sentence with a period

62.____

63. A. NO CHANGE
    B. tours, unfortunately, were
    C. tours unfortunately, were
    D. tours, unfortunately, are

63.____

64. A. NO CHANGE
    B. So
    C. But
    D. Therefore,

64.____

65. A. NO CHANGE
    B. He avoided discussing
    C. Having avoided discussing
    D. Upon avoiding the discussion of

65.____

66. A. NO CHANGE
    B. over
    C. on
    D. of

66.____

Questions 67-75.

DIRECTIONS: Questions 67 through 75 are based on the following passage.

Shooting rapids is not the only way to experience the thrill of canoeing. $\underset{67}{\underline{An}}$ ordinary-look-

ing stream, innocent of rocks and white water, can provide adventure, as long as it has three

essential $\underset{68}{\underline{features;}}$ a swift current, close banks, and $\underset{69}{\underline{has}}$ plenty of twists and turns.

$\underset{70}{\underline{A}}$ powerful current causes tension, for canoeists know they will have only seconds for

executing the maneuvers necessary to prevent crashing into the trees lining the narrow

$\underset{71}{\underline{streams\ banks.}}$ Of course, the $\underset{72}{\underline{narrowness,\ itself,\ being}}$ crucial in creating the tension. On a

broad stream, canoeists can pause frequently, catch their breath, and get their bearings. How-

ever, $\underset{73}{\underline{to}}$ a narrow stream, where every minute $\underset{74}{\underline{you\ run}}$ the risk of being knocked down by a

low-hanging tree limb, they must be constantly alert. Yet even the fast current and close banks
would be manageable if the stream were fairly straight. The expenditure of energy required to
paddle furiously, first on one side of the canoe and then on the other, wearies

$\underset{75}{\underline{both\ the\ nerves\ as\ well\ as\ the\ body.}}$

67. A. NO CHANGE
    B. They say that for adventure an
    C. Many finding that an
    D. The old saying that an

67._____

68. A. NO CHANGE
    B. features:
    C. features,
    D. features; these being

68._____

69. A. NO CHANGE
    B. there must be
    C. with
    D. OMIT the underlined portion

69._____

70. A. NO CHANGE
    B. Thus, a
    C. Therefore, a
    D. Furthermore, a

70._____

71. A. NO CHANGE
    B. stream's banks.
    C. streams bank's.
    D. banks of the streams.

71._____

72. A. NO CHANGE
    B. narrowness, itself is
    C. narrowness itself is
    D. narrowness in itself being

72._____

73. A. NO CHANGE
    B. near
    C. on
    D. with

73.____

74. A. NO CHANGE
    B. the canoer runs
    C. one runs
    D. they run

74.____

75. A. NO CHANGE
    B. the nerves as well as the body
    C. the nerves, also, as well as the body
    D. not only the body but also the nerves as well

75.____

———

KEY (CORRECT ANSWERS)

1.	C	26.	C	51.	D
2.	A	27.	C	52.	B
3.	D	28.	B	53.	A
4.	A	29.	D	54.	A
5.	B	30.	C	55.	D
6.	B	31.	D	56.	D
7.	D	32.	B	57.	C
8.	B	33.	A	58.	C
9.	C	34.	D	59.	D
10.	D	35.	A	60.	B
11.	A	36.	D	61.	A
12.	A	37.	C	62.	D
13.	B	38.	D	63.	B
14.	C	39.	A	64.	C
15.	C	40.	B	65.	B
16.	A	41.	A	66.	C
17.	C	42.	C	67.	A
18.	D	43.	B	68.	B
19.	D	44.	C	69.	D
20.	C	45.	D	70.	A
21.	A	46.	A	71.	B
22.	B	47.	A	72.	C
23.	A	48.	B	73.	C
24.	C	49.	C	74.	D
25.	D	50.	D	75.	B

———

PREPARING WRITTEN MATERIALS

EXAMINATION SECTION
TEST 1

DIRECTIONS: Each of the following questions consists of a sentence which may be classified appropriately under one of the following four categories:
- A. Incorrect because of faulty grammar or sentence structure
- B. Incorrect because of faulty punctuation
- C. Incorrect because of faulty spelling or capitalization
- D. Correct

Examine each sentence carefully. Then, in the space at the right, print the letter preceding the best of the four alternatives suggested above. All incorrect sentences contain but one type of error. Consider a sentence correct if it contains none of the types of errors mentioned, even though there may be other correct ways of expressing the same thought.

1. The fire apparently started in the storeroom, which is usually locked. 1._____

2. On approaching the victim two bruises were noticed by this officer. 2._____

3. The officer, who was there examined the report with great care. 3._____

4. Each employee in the office had a separate desk. 4._____

5. Each employee in the office had a separate desk. 5._____

6. The suggested procedure is similar to the one now in use. 6._____

7. No one was more pleased with the new procedure than the chauffeur. 7._____

8. He tried to pursuade her to change the procedure. 8._____

9. The total of the expenses charged to petty cash were high. 9._____

10. An understanding between him and I was finally reached. 10._____

11. It was at the supervisor's request that the clerk agreed to postpone his vacation. 11._____

12. We do not believe that it is necessary for both he and the clerk to attend the conference. 12._____

13. All employees, who display perseverance, will be given adequate recognition. 13._____

14. He regrets that some of us employees are dissatisfied with our new assignments. 14._____

15. "Do you think that the raise was merited," asked the supervisor? 15._____

16. The new manual of procedure is a valuable supplament to our rules and regulation. 16._____

17. The typist admitted that she had attempted to pursuade the other employees to assist her in her work. 17._____

18. The supervisor asked that all amendments to the regulations be handled by you and I. 18._____

19. They told both he and I that the prisoner had escaped. 19._____

20. Any superior officer, who, disregards the just complaints of his subordinates, is remiss in the performance of his duty. 20._____

21. Only those members of the national organization who resided in the Middle west attended the conference in Chicago. 21._____

22. We told him to give the investigation assignment to whoever was available. 22._____

23. Please do not disappoint and embarass us by not appearing in court. 23._____

24. Despite the efforts of the Supervising mechanic, the elevator could not be started. 24._____

25. The U.S. Weather Bureau, weather record for the accident date was checked. 25._____

KEY (CORRECT ANSWERS)

1.	D	11.	D
2.	A	12.	A
3.	B	13.	B
4.	D	14.	D
5.	B	15.	B
6.	C	16.	C
7.	D	17.	C
8.	C	18.	A
9.	A	19.	A
10.	A	20.	B

21.	C
22.	D
23.	C
24.	C
25.	B

TEST 2

DIRECTIONS: Each question consists of a sentence. Some of the sentences contain errors in English grammar or usage, punctuation, spelling, or capitalization. A sentence does not contain an error simply because it could be written in a different manner. Choose answer

    A. If the sentence contains an error in English grammar or usage
    B. If the sentence contains an error in punctuation
    C. If the sentence contains an error in spelling or capitalization
    D. If the sentence does not contain any errors.

1. The severity of the sentence prescribed by contemporary statutes - including both the former and the revised New York Penal Laws - do not depend on what crime was intended by the offender.

    1._____

2. It is generally recognized that two defects in the early law of attempt played a part in the birth of burglary: (1) immunity from prosecution for conduct short of the last act before completion of the crime, and (2) the relatively minor penalty imposed for an attempt (it being a common law misdemeanor) vis-a-vis the completed offense.

    2._____

3. The first sentence of the statute is applicable to employees who enter their place of employment, invited guests, and all other persons who have an express or implied license or privilege to enter the premises.

    3._____

4. Contemporary criminal codes in the United States generally divide burglary into various degrees, differentiating the categories according to place, time and other attendent circumstances.

    4._____

5. The assignment was completed in record time but the payroll for it has not yet been preparid.

    5._____

6. The operator, on the other hand, is willing to learn me how to use the mimeograph.

    6._____

7. She is the prettiest of the three sisters.

    7._____

8. She doesn't know; if the mail has arrived.

    8._____

9. The doorknob of the office door is broke.

    9._____

10. Although the department's supply of scratch pads and stationery have diminished considerably, the allotment for our division has not been reduced.

    10._____

11. You have not told us whom you wish to designate as your secretary.

    11._____

12. Upon reading the minutes of the last meeting, the new proposal was taken up for consideration.

    12._____

13. Before beginning the discussion, we locked the door as a precautionery measure.

    13._____

14. The supervisor remarked, "Only those clerks, who perform routine work, are permitted to take a rest period."

    14._____

15. Not only will this duplicating machine make accurate copies, but it will also produce a quantity of work equal to fifteen transcribing typists.

    15._____

16. "Mr. Jones," said the supervisor, "we regret our inability to grant you an extent ion of your leave of absence." 16.____

17. Although the employees find the work monotonous and fatigueing, they rarely complain. 17.____

18. We completed the tabulation of the receipts on time despite the fact that Miss Smith our fastest operator was absent for over a week. 18.____

19. The reaction of the employees who attended the meeting, as well as the reaction of those who did not attend, indicates clearly that the schedule is satisfactory to everyone concerned. 19.____

20. Of the two employees, the one in our office is the most efficient. 20.____

21. No one can apply or even understand, the new rules and regulations. 21.____

22. A large amount of supplies were stored in the empty office. 22.____

23. If an employee is occassionally asked to work overtime, he should do so willingly. 23.____

24. It is true that the new procedures are difficult to use but, we are certain that you will learn them quickly. 24.____

25. The office manager said that he did not know who would be given a large allotment under the new plan. 25.____

KEY (CORRECT ANSWERS)

1.	A	11.	D
2.	D	12.	A
3.	D	13.	C
4.	C	14.	B
5.	C	15.	A
6.	A	16.	C
7.	D	17.	C
8.	B	18.	B
9.	A	19.	D
10.	A	20.	A

21.	B
22.	A
23.	C
24.	B
25.	D

TEST 3

DIRECTIONS: Each of the following sentences may be classified MOST appropriately under one of the following our categories:
- A. faulty because of incorrect grammar;
- B. faulty because of incorrect punctuation;
- C. faulty because of incorrect capitalization;
- D. correct

Examine each sentence carefully. Then, in the space at the right, print the capital letter preceding the option which is the BEST of the four suggested above. All incorrect sentences contain but one type of error. Consider a sentence correct if it contains none of the types of errors mentioned, even though there may be other correct ways of expressing the same thought.

1. The desk, as well as the chairs, were moved out of the office.   1.____

2. The clerk whose production was greatest for the month won a day's vacation as first prize.   2.____

3. Upon entering the room, the employees were found hard at work at their desks.   3.____

4. John Smith our new employee always arrives at work on time.   4.____

5. Punish whoever is guilty of stealing the money.   5.____

6. Intelligent and persistent effort lead to success no matter what the job may be.   6.____

7. The secretary asked, "can you call again at three o'clock?"   7.____

8. He told us, that if the report was not accepted at the next meeting, it would have to be rewritten.   8.____

9. He would not have sent the letter if he had known that it would cause so much excitement.   9.____

10. We all looked forward to him coming to visit us.   10.____

11. If you find that you are unable to complete the assignment please notify me as soon as possible.   11.____

12. Every girl in the office went home on time but me; there was still some work for me to finish.   12.____

13. He wanted to know who the letter was addressed to, Mr. Brown or Mr. Smith.   13.____

14. "Mr. Jones, he said, please answer this letter as soon as possible."   14.____

15. The new clerk had an unusual accent inasmuch as he was born and educated in the south.   15.____

16. Although he is younger than her, he earns a higher salary.   16.____

17. Neither of the two administrators are going to attend the conference being held in Washington, D.C. 17.____

18. Since Miss Smith and Miss Jones have more experience than us, they have been given more responsible duties. 18.____

19. Mr. Shaw the supervisor of the stock room maintains an inventory of stationery and office supplies. 19.____

20. Inasmuch as this matter affects both you and I, we should take joint action. 20.____

21. Who do you think will be able to perform this highly technical work? 21.____

22. Of the two employees, John is considered the most competent. 22.____

23. He is not coming home on tuesday; we expect him next week. 23.____

24. Stenographers, as well as typists must be able to type rapidly and accurately. 24.____

25. Having been placed in the safe we were sure that the money would not be stolen. 25.____

KEY (CORRECT ANSWERS)

1.	A	11.	B
2.	D	12.	D
3.	A	13.	A
4.	B	14.	B
5.	D	15.	C
6.	A	16.	A
7.	C	17.	A
8.	A	18.	A
9.	D	19.	B
10.	A	20.	A

21.	D
22.	A
23.	C
24.	B
25.	A

TEST 4

DIRECTIONS: Each of the following sentences consist of four sentences lettered A, B, C, and D. One of the sentences in each group contains an error in grammar or punctuation. Indicate the INCORRECT sentence in each group. *PRINT THE LETTER OF THE CORRECT ANSWER IN THE SPACE AT THE RIGHT.*

1. A. Give the message to whoever is on duty.
    B. The teacher who's pupil won first prize presented the award.
    C. Between you and me, I don't expect the program to succeed.
    D. His running to catch the bus caused the accident.

    1.____

2. A. The process, which was patented only last year is already obsolete.
    B. His interest in science (which continues to the present) led him to convert his basement into a laboratory.
    C. He described the book as "verbose, repetitious, and bombastic".
    D. Our new director will need to possess three qualities: vision, patience, and fortitude.

    2.____

3. A. The length of ladder trucks varies considerably.
    B. The probationary fireman reported to the officer to whom he was assigned.
    C. The lecturer emphasized the need for we firemen to be punctual.
    D. Neither the officers nor the members of the company knew about the new procedure.

    3.____

4. A. Ham and eggs is the specialty of the house.
    B. He is one of the students who are on probation.
    C. Do you think that either one of us have a chance to be nominated for president of the class?
    D. I assume that either he was to be in charge or you were.

    4.____

5. A. Its a long road that has no turn.
    B. To run is more tiring than to walk.
    C. We have been assigned three new reports: namely, the statistical summary, the narrative summary, and the budgetary summary.
    D. Had the first payment been made in January, the second would be due in April.

    5.____

6. A. Each employer has his own responsibilities.
    B. If a person speaks correctly, they make a good impression.
    C. Every one of the operators has had her vacation.
    D. Has anybody filed his report?

    6.____

7. A. The manager, with all his salesmen, was obliged to go.
    B. Who besides them is to sign the agreement?
    C. One report without the others is incomplete.
    D. Several clerks, as well as the proprietor, was injured.

    7.____

8. A. A suspension of these activities is expected.
    B. The machine is economical because first cost and upkeep are low.
    C. A knowledge of stenography and filing are required for this position.
    D. The condition in which the goods were received shows that the packing was not done properly.

    8.____

9. A. There seems to be a great many reasons for disagreement. 9._____
    B. It does not seem possible that they could have failed.
    C. Have there always been too few applicants for these positions?
    D. There is no excuse for these errors.

10. A. We shall be pleased to answer your question. 10._____
    B. Shall we plan the meeting for Saturday?
    C. I will call you promptly at seven.
    D. Can I borrow your book after you have read it?

11. A. You are as capable as I. 11._____
    B. Everyone is willing to sign but him and me.
    C. As for he and his assistant, I cannot praise them too highly.
    D. Between you and me, I think he will be dismissed.

12. A. Our competitors bid above us last week. 12._____
    B. The survey which was began last year has not yet been completed.
    C. The operators had shown that they understood their instructions.
    D. We have never ridden over worse roads.

13. A. Who did they say was responsible? 13._____
    B. Whom did you suspect?
    C. Who do you suppose it was?
    D. Whom do you mean?

14. A. Of the two propositions, this is the worse. 14._____
    B. Which report do you consider the best -- the one in January or the one in July?
    C. I believe this is the most practicable of the many plans submitted.
    D. He is the youngest employee in the organization.

15. A. The firm had but three orders last week. 15._____
    B. That doesn't really seem possible.
    C. After twenty years scarcely none of the old business remains.
    D. Has he done nothing about it?

KEY (CORRECT ANSWERS)

1.	B		6.	B
2.	A		7.	D
3.	C		8.	C
4.	C		9.	A
5.	A		10.	D

11.	C
12.	B
13.	A
14.	B
15.	C

PREPARING WRITTEN MATERIAL

EXAMINATION SECTION
TEST 1

DIRECTIONS: Each question or incomplete statement is followed by several suggested answers or completions. Select the one that BEST answers the question or completes the statement. *PRINT THE LETTER OF THE CORRECT ANSWER IN THE SPACE AT THE RIGHT.*

Questions 1-4.

DIRECTIONS: Questions 1 through 4 each consist of a sentence which may or may not be an example of good English. The underlined parts of each sentence may be correct or incorrect. Examine each sentence, considering grammar, punctuation, spelling, and capitalization. If the English usage in the underlined parts of the sentence given is better than any of the changes in the underlined words suggested in options B, C, or D, choose option A. If the changes in the underlined words suggested in options B, C, or D would make the sentence correct, choose the correct option. Do not choose an option that will change the meaning of the sentence.

1. This <u>Fall</u>, the office will be closed on <u>Columbus Day, October</u> 9th.   1.____

    A. Correct as is
    B. fall...Columbus Day, October
    C. Fall...columbus day, October
    D. fall...Columbus Day, October

2. There <u>weren't no</u> paper in the supply closet.   2.____

    A. Correct as is   B. weren't any
    C. wasn't any   D. wasn't no

3. The <u>alphabet, or A to Z sequence are</u> the basis of most filing systems.   3.____

    A. Correct as is
    B. alphabet, or A to Z sequence, is
    C. alphabet, or A to Z sequence, are
    D. alphabet, or A too Z sequence, is

4. The Office Aide checked the <u>register and finding</u> the date of the meeting.   4.____

    A. Correct as is   B. regaster and finding
    C. register and found   D. regaster and found

Questions 5-10.

DIRECTIONS: Questions 5 through 10 consist of sentences which contain examples of correct or incorrect English usage. Examine each sentence with reference to grammar, spelling, punctuation, and capitalization. Choose one of the following options that would be BEST for correct English usage:

A. The sentence is correct
B. There is one mistake
C. There are two mistakes
D. There are three mistakes

5. Mrs. Fitzgerald came to the 59th Precinct to retreive her property which were stolen earlier in the week.   5.____

6. The two officer's responded to the call, only to find that the perpatrator and the victim have left the scene.   6.____

7. Mr. Coleman called the 61st Precinct to report that, upon arriving at his store, he discovered that there was a large hole in the wall and that three boxes of radios were missing.   7.____

8. The Administrative Leiutenant of the 62nd Precinct held a meeting which was attended by all the civilians, assigned to the Precinct.   8.____

9. Three days after the robbery occured the detective apprahended two suspects and recovered the stolen items.   9.____

10. The Community Affairs Officer of the 64th Precinct is the liaison between the Precinct and the community; he works closely with various community organizations, and elected officials.   10.____

Questions 11-18.

DIRECTIONS: Questions 11 through 18 are to be answered on the basis of the following paragraph, which contains some deliberate errors in spelling and/or grammar and/or punctuation. Each line of the paragraph is preceded by a number. There are 9 lines and 9 numbers.

Line No.	Paragraph Line
1	The protection of life and proporty are, one of
2	the oldest and most important functions of a city.
3	New York city has it's own full-time police Agency.
4	The police Department has the power an it shall
5	be there duty to preserve the Public piece,
6	prevent crime detect and arrest offenders, supress
7	riots, protect the rites of persons and property, etc.
8	The maintainance of sound relations with the community they
9	serve is an important function of law enforcement officers

11. How many errors are contained in line one?   11.____

    A. One   B. Two   C. Three   D. None

12. How many errors are contained in line two?   12.____

    A. One   B. Two   C. Three   D. None

13. How many errors are contained in line three?   13.____

    A. One   B. Two   C. Three   D. None

14. How many errors are contained in line four?   14._____

    A. One   B. Two   C. Three   D. None

15. How many errors are contained in line five?   15._____

    A. One   B. Two   C. Three   D. None

16. How many errors are contained in line six?   16._____

    A. One   B. Two   C. Three   D. None

17. How many errors are contained in line seven?   17._____

    A. One   B. Two   C. Three   D. None

18. How many errors are contained in line eight?   18._____

    A. One   B. Two   C. Three   D. None

19. In the sentence, *The candidate wants to file his application for preference before it is too*   19._____
late, the word *before* is used as a(n)

    A. preposition   B. subordinating conjunction
    C. pronoun   D. adverb

20. The one of the following sentences which is grammatically PREFERABLE to the others   20._____
is:

    A. Our engineers will go over your blueprints so that you may have no problems in construction.
    B. For a long time he had been arguing that we, not he, are to blame for the confusion.
    C. I worked on this automobile for two hours and still cannot find out what is wrong with it.
    D. Accustomed to all kinds of hardships, fatigue seldom bothers veteran policemen.

KEY (CORRECT ANSWERS)

1.	A	11.	C
2.	C	12.	D
3.	B	13.	C
4.	C	14.	B
5.	C	15.	C
6.	D	16.	B
7.	A	17.	A
8.	C	18.	A
9.	C	19.	B
10.	B	20.	A

TEST 2

DIRECTIONS: Each question or incomplete statement is followed by several suggested answers or completions. Select the one that BEST answers the question or completes the statement. *PRINT THE LETTER OF THE CORRECT ANSWER IN THE SPACE AT THE RIGHT.*

1. The plural of   1.____

    A. turkey is turkies
    B. cargo is cargoes
    C. bankruptcy is bankruptcys
    D. son-in-law is son-in-laws

2. The abbreviation *viz.* means MOST NEARLY   2.____

    A. namely   B. for example
    C. the following   D. see

3. In the sentence, *A man in a light-grey suit waited thirty-five minutes in the ante-room for the all-important document,* the word IMPROPERLY hyphenated is   3.____

    A. light-grey   B. thirty-five
    C. ante-room   D. all-important

4. The MOST accurate of the following sentences is: 4.____

    A. The commissioner, as well as his deputy and various bureau heads, were present.
    B. A new organization of employers and employees have been formed.
    C. One or the other of these men have been selected.
    D. The number of pages in the book is enough to discourage a reader.

5. The MOST accurate of the following sentences is: 5.____

    A. Between you and me, I think he is the better man.
    B. He was believed to be me.
    C. Is it us that you wish to see?
    D. The winners are him and her.

Questions 6-13.

DIRECTIONS: The sentences numbered 6 through 13 deal with some phase of police activity. They may be classified most appropriately under one of the following four categories.
    A. Faulty because of incorrect grammar
    B. Faulty because of incorrect punctuation
    C. Faulty because of incorrect use of a word
    D. Correct

Examine each sentence carefully. Then, in the space at the right, print the capital letter preceding the option which is the BEST of the four suggested above. All incorrect sentences contain only one type of error. Consider a sentence correct if it contains none of the types of errors mentioned, even though there may be other correct ways of expressing the same thought.

6. The Department Medal of Honor is awarded to a member of the Police Force who distin-guishes himself inconspicuously in the line of police duty by the performance of an act of gallantry.

6.____

7. Members of the Detective Division are charged with the prevention of crime, the detec-tion and arrest of criminals and the recovery of lost or stolen property.

7.____

8. Detectives are selected from the uniformed patrol forces after they have indicated by conduct, aptitude and performance that they are qualified for the more intricate duties of a detective.

8.____

9. The patrolman, pursuing his assailant, exchanged shots with the gunman and immortally wounded him as he fled into a nearby building.

9.____

10. The members of the Traffic Division has to enforce the Vehicle and Traffic Law, the Traffic Regulations and ordinances relating to vehicular and pedestrian traffic.

10.____

11. After firing a shot at the gunman, the crowd dispersed from the patrolman's line of fire.

11.____

12. The efficiency of the Missing Persons Bureau is maintained with a maximum of public personnel due to the specialized training given to its members.

12.____

13. Records of persons arrested for violations of Vehicle and Traffic Regulations are trans-mitted upon request to precincts, courts and other authorized agencies.

13.____

14. Following are two sentences which may or may not be written in correct English:
     I.   Two clients assaulted the officer.
    II.   The van is illegally parked.
Which one of the following statements is CORRECT?

14.____

   A.   Only Sentence I is written in correct English.
   B.   Only Sentence II is written in correct English.
   C.   Sentences I and II are both written in correct English.
   D.   Neither Sentence I nor Sentence II is written in correct English.

15. Following are two sentences which may or may not be written in correct English:
     I.   Security Officer Rollo escorted the visitor to the patrolroom.
    II.   Two entry were made in the facility logbook.
Which one of the following statements is CORRECT?

15.____

   A.   Only Sentence I is written in correct English.
   B.   Only Sentence II is written in correct English.
   C.   Sentences I and II are both written in correct English.
   D.   Neither Sentence I nor Sentence II is written in correct English.

16. Following are two sentences which may or may not be written in correct English:
     I.   Officer McElroy putted out a small fire in the wastepaper basket.
    II.   Special Officer Janssen told the visitor where he could obtained a pass.
Which one of the following statements is CORRECT?

16.____

   A.   Only Sentence I is written in correct English.
   B.   Only Sentence II is written in correct English.
   C.   Sentences I and II are both written in correct English.
   D.   Neither Sentence I nor Sentence II is written in correct English.

17. Following are two sentences which may or may not be written in correct English: 17.____
    I.   Security Officer Warren observed a broken window while he was on his post in Hallway C.
    II.   The worker reported that two typewriters had been stoled from the office.
Which one of the following statements is CORRECT?

    A.   Only Sentence I is written in correct English.
    B.   Only Sentence II is written in correct English.
    C.   Sentences I and II are both written in correct English.
    D.   Neither Sentence I nor Sentence II is written in correct English.

18. Following are two sentences which may or may not be written in correct English: 18.____
    I.   Special Officer Cleveland was attempting to calm an emotionally disturbed visitor.
    II.   The visitor did not stops crying and calling for his wife.
Which one of the following statements is CORRECT?

    A.   Only Sentence I is written in correct English.
    B.   Only Sentence II is written in correct English.
    C.   Sentences I and II are both written in correct English.
    D.   Neither Sentence I nor Sentence II is written in correct English.

19. Following are two sentences that may or may not be written in correct English: 19.____
    I.   While on patrol, I observes a vagrant loitering near the drug dispensary.
    II.   I escorted the vagrant out of the building and off the premises.
Which one of the following statements is CORRECT?

    A.   Only Sentence I is written in correct English.
    B.   Only Sentence II is written in correct English.
    C.   Sentences I and II are both written in correct English.
    D.   Neither Sentence I nor Sentence II is written in correct English.

20. Following are two sentences which may or may not be written in correct English: 20.____
    I.   At 4:00 P.M., Sergeant Raymond told me to evacuate the waiting area immediately due to a bomb threat.
    II.   Some of the clients did not want to leave the building.
Which one of the following statements is CORRECT?

    A.   Only Sentence I is written in correct English.
    B.   Only Sentence II is written in correct English.
    C.   Sentences I and II are both written in correct English.
    D.   Neither Sentence I nor Sentence II is written in correct English.

KEY (CORRECT ANSWERS)

1.	B		11.	A
2.	A		12.	C
3.	C		13.	D
4.	D		14.	C
5.	A		15.	A
6.	C		16.	D
7.	B		17.	A
8.	D		18.	A
9.	C		19.	B
10.	A		20.	C

———

READING COMPREHENSION
UNDERSTANDING AND INTERPRETING WRITTEN MATERIAL
EXAMINATION SECTION
TEST 1

DIRECTIONS   Each question or incomplete statement is followed by several suggested answers or completions. Select the one that BEST answers the question or completes the statement. *PRINT THE LETTER OF THE CORRECT ANSWER IN THE SPACE AT THE RIGHT.*

Questions 1-8.

DIRECTIONS: Questions 1 through 8 are to be answered on the basis of the following regulations governing Newspaper Carriers when on subway trains or station platforms. These Newspaper Carriers are issued badges which entitle them to enter subway stations, when carrying papers in accordance with these regulations, without paying a fare.

REGULATIONS GOVERNING NEWSPAPER CARRIERS
WHEN ON SUBWAY TRAINS OR STATION PLATFORMS

1. Carriers must wear badges at all times when on trains.
2. Carriers must not sort, separate, or wrap bundles on trains or insert sections.
3. Carriers must not obstruct platform of cars or stations.
4. Carriers may make delivery to stands inside the stations by depositing their badge with the station agent.
5. Throwing of bundles is strictly prohibited and will be cause for arrest.
6. Each bundle must not be over 18" x 12" x 15".
7. Not more than two bundles shall be carried by each carrier. (An extra fare to be charged for a second bundle.)
8. No wire to be used on bundles carried into stations.

1. These regulations do NOT prohibit carriers on trains from _____ newspapers.   1.____

    A. sorting bundles of   B. carrying bundles of
    C. wrapping bundles of   D. inserting sections into

2. A carrier delivering newspapers to a stand inside of the station MUST   2.____

    A. wear his badge at all times
    B. leave his badge with the railroad clerk
    C. show his badge to the railroad clerk
    D. show his badge at the newsstand

3. Carriers are warned against throwing bundles of newspapers from trains MAINLY because these acts may   3.____

    A. wreck the stand   B. cause injury to passengers
    C. hurt the carrier   D. damage the newspaper

4. It is permissible for a carrier to temporarily leave his bundles of newspapers   4.____

    A. near the subway car's door
    B. at the foot of the station stairs
    C. in front of the exit gate
    D. on a station bench

5. Of the following, the carrier who should NOT be restricted from entering the subway is   5.____
the one carrying a bundle which is _____long, _____ wide, and _____ high.

    A. 15"; 18"; 18"   B. 18"; 12"; 18"
    C. 18"; 12"; 15"   D. 18"; 15"; 15"

6. A carrier who will have to pay one fare is carrying _____ bundle(s).   6.____

    A. one   B. two   C. three   D. four

7. Wire may NOT be used for tying bundles because it may be   7.____

    A. rusty
    B. expensive
    C. needed for other purposes
    D. dangerous to other passengers

8. If a carrier is arrested in violation of these regulations, the PROBABLE reason is that he   8.____

    A. carried too many papers
    B. was not wearing his badge
    C. separated bundles of newspapers on the train
    D. tossed a bundle of newspapers to a carrier on a train

Questions 9-12.

DIRECTIONS: Questions 9 through 12 are to be answered on the basis of the Bulletin printed below. Read this Bulletin carefully before answering these questions. Select your answers ONLY on the basis of this Bulletin.

BULLETIN

Rule 107(m) states, in part, that *Before closing doors they (Conductors) must afford passengers an opportunity to detrain and entrain...*

Doors must be left open long enough to allow passengers to enter and exit from the train. Closing doors on passengers too quickly does not help to shorten the station stop and is a violation of the safety and courtesy which must be accorded to all our passengers.

The proper and effective way to keep passengers moving in and out of the train is to use the public address system. When the train is excessively crowded and passengers on the platform are pushing those in the cars, it may be necessary to close the doors after a reasonable period of time has been allowed.

Closing doors on passengers too quickly is a violation of rules and will be cause for disciplinary actions.

9. Which of the following statements is CORRECT about closing doors on passengers too quickly? It   9.____

    A. will shorten the running time from terminal to terminal
    B. shortens the station stop but is a violation of safety and courtesy
    C. does not help shorten the station stop time
    D. makes the passengers detrain and entrain quicker

10. The BEST way to get passengers to move in and out of cars quickly is to   10.____

    A. have the platform conductors urge passengers to move into doorways
    B. make announcements over the public address system
    C. start closing doors while passengers are getting on
    D. set a fixed time for stopping at each station

11. The conductor should leave doors open at each station stop long enough for passengers to   11.____

    A. squeeze into an excessively crowded train
    B. get from the local to the express train
    C. get off and get on the train
    D. hear the announcements over the public address system

12. Closing doors on passengers too quickly is a violation of rules and is cause for   12.____

    A. the conductor's immediate suspension
    B. the conductor to be sent back to the terminal for another assignment
    C. removal of the conductor at the next station
    D. disciplinary action to be taken against the conductor

Questions 13-15.

DIRECTIONS: Questions 13 through 15 are to be answered on the basis of the Bulletin printed below. Read this Bulletin carefully before answering these questions. Select your answers ONLY on the basis of this Bulletin.

BULLETIN

Conductors assigned to train service are not required to wear uniform caps from June 1 to September 30, inclusive.

Conductors assigned to platform duty are required to wear the uniform cap at all times. Conductors are reminded that they must furnish their badge numbers to anyone who requests same.

During the above-mentioned period, conductors may remove their uniform coats. The regulation summer short-sleeved shirts must be worn with the regulation uniform trousers. Suspenders are not permitted if the uniform coat is removed. Shoes are to be black but sandals, sneakers, suede, canvas, or two-tone footwear must not be worn.

Conductors may work without uniform tie if the uniform coat is removed. However, only the top collar button may be opened. The tie may not be removed if the uniform coat is worn.

13. Conductors assigned to platform duty are required to wear uniform caps   13.____

    A. at all times except from June 1 to September 30, inclusive
    B. whenever they are on duty
    C. only from June 1 to September 30, inclusive
    D. only when they remove their uniform coats

14. Suspenders are permitted ONLY if conductors wear   14.____

    A. summer short-sleeved shirts with uniform trousers
    B. uniform trousers without belt loops
    C. the type permitted by the authority
    D. uniform coats

15. A conductor MUST furnish his badge number to   15.____

    A. authority supervisors only
    B. members of special inspection only
    C. anyone who asks him for it
    D. passengers only

Questions 16-17.

DIRECTIONS: Questions 16 and 17 are to be answered SOLELY on the basis of the following Bulletin.

BULLETIN

Effective immediately, Conductors on trains equipped with public address systems shall make the following announcements in addition to their regular station announcement. At stations where passengers normally board trains from their homes or places of employment, the announcement shall be *Good Morning* or *Good Afternoon* or *Good Evening,* depending on the time of the day. At stations where passengers normally leave trains for their homes or places of employment, the announcement shall be *Have a Good Day* or *Good Night,* depending on the time of day or night.

16. The MAIN purpose of making the additional announcements mentioned in the Bulletin is   16.____
MOST likely to

    A. keep passengers informed about the time of day
    B. determine whether the public address system works in case of an emergency
    C. make the passengers' ride more pleasant
    D. have the conductor get used to using the public address system

17. According to this Bulletin, a conductor should greet passengers boarding the *D* train at   17.____
the Coney Island Station at 8 A.M. Monday by announcing

    A. Have a Good Day
    B. Good Morning
    C. Watch your step as you leave
    D. Good Evening

Questions 18-25.

DIRECTIONS: Questions 18 through 25 are to be answered on the basis of the information
regarding the incident given below. Read this information carefully before
answering these questions.

INCIDENT

As John Brown, a cleaner, was sweeping the subway station platform, in accordance with
his assigned schedule, he was accused by Henry Adams of unnecessarily bumping him with
the broom and scolded for doing this work when so many passengers were on the platform.
Adams obtained Brown's badge number and stated that he would report the matter to the
Transit Authority. Standing around and watching this were Mary Smith, a schoolteacher, Ann
Jones, a student, and Joe Black, a maintainer, with Jim Roe, his helper, who had been working on one of the turnstiles. Brown thereupon proceeded to take the names and addresses of
these people as required by the Transit Authority rule which directs that names and
addresses of as many disinterested witnesses be taken as possible. Shortly thereafter, a train
arrived at the station and Adams, as well as several other people, boarded the train and left.
Brown went back to his work of sweeping the station.

18. The cleaner was sweeping the station at this time because   18.____

    A. the platform was unusually dirty
    B. there were very few passengers on the platform
    C. he had no regard for the passengers
    D. it was set by his work schedule

19. This incident proves that   19.____

    A. witnesses are needed in such cases
    B. porters are generally careless
    C. subway employees stick together
    D. brooms are dangerous in the subway

20. Joe Black was a   20.____

    A. helper   B. maintainer
    C. cleaner   D. teacher

21. The number of persons witnessing this incident was   21.____

    A. 2   B. 3   C. 4   D. 5

22. The addresses of witnesses are required so that they may later be   22.____

    A. depended on to testify   B. recognized
    C. paid   D. located

23. The person who said he would report this incident to the transit authority was   23.____

    A. Black   B. Adams   C. Brown   D. Roe

24. The ONLY person of the following who positively did NOT board the train was   24.____

    A. Brown   B. Smith   C. Adams   D. Jones

25. As a result of this incident,   25.____

    A. no action need be taken against the cleaner unless Adams makes a written complaint
    B. the cleaner should be given the rest of the day off
    C. the handles of the brooms used should be made shorter
    D. Brown's badge number should be changed

_____

KEY (CORRECT ANSWERS)

1.	B		11.	C
2.	B		12.	D
3.	B		13.	B
4.	D		14.	D
5.	C		15.	C
6.	A		16.	C
7.	D		17.	B
8.	D		18.	D
9.	C		19.	A
10.	B		20.	B

21.	C
22.	D
23.	B
24.	A
25.	A

_____

TEST 2

DIRECTIONS: Each question or incomplete statement is followed by several suggested answers or completions. Select the one that BEST answers the question or completes the statement. *PRINT THE LETTER OF THE CORRECT ANSWER IN THE SPACE AT THE RIGHT.*

Questions 1-10.

DIRECTIONS: Questions 1 through 10 are to be answered on the basis of the information contained in the following safety rules. Read the rules carefully before answering these questions.

SAFETY RULES

Employees must take every precaution to prevent accidents, or injury to persons, or damage to property. For this reason, they must observe conditions of the equipment and tools with which they work, and the structures upon which they work.

It is the duty of all employees to report to their superior all dangerous conditions which they may observe. Employees must use every precaution to prevent the origin of fire. If they discover smoke or a fire in the subway, they shall proceed to the nearest telephone and notify the trainmaster giving their name, badge number, and location of the trouble.

In case of accidents on the subway system, employees must, if possible, secure the name, address, and telephone number of any passengers who may have been injured.

Employees at or near the location of trouble on the subway system, whether it be a fire or an accident, shall render all practical assistance which they are qualified to perform.

1. The BEST way for employees to prevent an accident is to   1._____

   A. secure the names of the injured persons
   B. arrive promptly at the location of the accident
   C. give their name and badge numbers to the trainmaster
   D. take all necessary precautions

2. In case of trouble, trackmen are NOT expected to   2._____

   A. report fires
   B. give help if they don't know how
   C. secure telephone numbers of persons injured in subway accidents
   D. give their badge number to anyone

3. Trackmen MUST   3._____

   A. be present at all fires
   B. see all accidents
   C. report dangerous conditions
   D. be the first to discover smoke in the subway

4. Observing conditions means to

    A. look at things carefully
    B. report what you see
    C. ignore things that are none of your business
    D. correct dangerous conditions

4.____

5. A dangerous condition existing on the subway system which a trackman should observe and report to his superior would be

    A. passengers crowding into trains
    B. trains running behind schedule
    C. tools in defective condition
    D. some newspapers on the track

5.____

6. If a trackman discovers a badly worn rail, he should

    A. not take any action
    B. remove the worn section of rail
    C. notify his superior
    D. replace the rail

6.____

7. The MAIN reason a trackman should observe the condition of his tools is

    A. so that they won't be stolen
    B. because they don't belong to him
    C. to prevent accidents
    D. because they cannot be replaced

7.____

8. If a passenger who paid his fare is injured in a subway accident, it is MOST important that an employee obtain the passenger's

    A. name   B. age
    C. badge number   D. destination

8.____

9. An employee who happens to be at the scene of an accident on a crowded station of the system should

    A. not give assistance unless he chooses to do so
    B. leave the scene immediately
    C. question all bystanders
    D. render whatever assistance he can

9.____

10. If a trackman discovers a fire at one end of a station platform and telephones the information to the trainmaster, he need NOT give

    A. the trainmaster's name
    B. the name of the station involved
    C. his own name
    D. the number of his badge

10.____

Questions 11-15.

DIRECTIONS: Questions 11 through 15 are to be answered on the basis of the information contained in the safety regulations given below. Refer to these rules in answering these questions.

REGULATIONS FOR SMALL GROUPS WHO
MOVE FROM POINT TO POINT ON THE TRACKS

Employees who perform duties on the tracks in small groups and who move from point to point along the trainway must be on the alert at all times and prepared to clear the track when a train approaches without unnecessarily slowing it down. Underground at all times, and out-of-doors between sunset and sunrise, such employees must not enter upon the tracks unless each of them is equipped with an approved light. Flashlights must not be used for protection by such groups. Upon clearing the track to permit a train to pass, each member of the group must give a proceed signal, by hand or light, to the motorman of the train. Whenever such small groups are working in an area protected by caution lights or flags, but are not members of the gang for whom the flagging protection was established, they must not give proceed signals to motormen. The purpose of this rule is to avoid a motorman's confusing such signal with that of the flagman who is protecting a gang. Whenever a small group is engaged in work of an engrossing nature or at any time when the view of approaching trains is limited by reason of curves or otherwise, one man of the group, equipped with a whistle, must be assigned properly to warn and protect the man or men at work and must not perform any other duties while so assigned.

11. If a small group of men are traveling along the tracks toward their work location and a train approaches, they should

    A. stop the train
    B. signal the motorman to go slowly
    C. clear the track
    D. stop immediately

11.____

12. Small groups may enter upon the tracks

    A. only between sunset and sunrise
    B. provided each has an approved light
    C. provided their foreman has a good flashlight
    D. provided each man has an approved flashlight

12.____

13. After a small group has cleared the tracks in an area unprotected by caution lights or flags,

    A. each member must give the proceed signal to the motorman
    B. the foreman signals the motorman to proceed
    C. the motorman can proceed provided he goes slowly
    D. the last member off the tracks gives the signal to the motorman

13.____

14. If a small group is working in an area protected by the signals of a track gang, the members of the small group

    A. need not be concerned with train movement
    B. must give the proceed signal together with the track gang

14.____

C. can delegate one of their members to give the proceed signal
D. must not give the proceed signal

15. If the view of approaching trains is blocked, the small group should   15.____

    A. move to where they can see the trains
    B. delegate one of the group to warn and protect them
    C. keep their ears alert for approaching trains
    D. refuse to work at such locations

Questions 16-25.

DIRECTIONS: Questions 16 through 25 are to be answered SOLELY on the basis of the article about general safety precautions given below.

GENERAL SAFETY PRECAUTIONS

When work is being done on or next to a track on which regular trains are running, special signals must be displayed as called for in the general rules for flagging. Yellow caution signals, green clear signals, and a flagman with a red danger signal are required for the protection of traffic and workmen in accordance with the standard flagging rules. The flagman shall also carry a white signal for display to the motorman when he may proceed. The foreman in charge must see that proper signals are displayed.

On elevated lines during daylight hours, the yellow signal shall be a yellow flag, the red signal shall be a red flag, the green signal shall be a green flag, and the white signal shall be a white flag. In subway sections, and on elevated lines after dark, the yellow signal shall be a yellow lantern, the red signal shall be a red lantern, the green signal shall be a green lantern, and the white signal shall be a white lantern.

Caution and clear signals are to be secured to the elevated or subway structure with non-metallic fastenings outside the clearance line of the train and on the motorman's side of the track.

16. On elevated lines during daylight hours, the caution signal is a   16.____

    A. yellow lantern   B. green lantern
    C. yellow flag   D. green flag

17. In subway sections, the clear signal is a   17.____

    A. yellow lantern   B. green lantern
    C. yellow flag   D. green flag

18. The MINIMUM number of lanterns that a subway track flagman should carry is   18.____

    A. 1   B. 2   C. 3   D. 4

19. The PRIMARY purpose of flagging is to protect the   19.____

    A. flagman   B. motorman
    C. track workers   D. railroad

20. A suitable fastening for securing caution lights to the elevated or subway structure is   20.____

    A. copper nails   B. steel wire
    C. brass rods   D. cotton twine

21. On elevated structures during daylight hours, the red flag is held by the   21.____

    A. motorman   B. foreman   C. trackman   D. flagman

22. The signal used in the subway to notify a motorman to proceed is a   22.____

    A. white lantern   B. green lantern
    C. red flag   D. yellow flag

23. The caution, clear, and danger signals are displayed for the information of   23.____

    A. trackmen   B. workmen   C. flagmen   D. motormen

24. Since the motorman's cab is on the right-hand side, caution signals should be secured to   24.____
    the

    A. right-hand running rail
    B. left-hand running rail
    C. structure to the right of the track
    D. structure to the left of the track

25. In a track work gang, the person responsible for the proper display of signals is the   25.____

    A. track worker   B. foreman
    C. motorman   D. flagman

KEY (CORRECT ANSWERS)

1.	D		11.	C
2.	B		12.	B
3.	C		13.	A
4.	A		14.	D
5.	C		15.	B
6.	C		16.	C
7.	C		17.	B
8.	A		18.	B
9.	D		19.	C
10.	A		20.	D

21. D
22. A
23. D
24. C
25. B

TEST 3

DIRECTIONS: Each question or incomplete statement is followed by several suggested answers or completions. Select the one that BEST answers the question or completes the statement. *PRINT THE LETTER OF THE CORRECT ANSWER IN THE SPACE AT THE RIGHT.*

Questions 1-6.

DIRECTIONS: Questions 1 through 6 are to be answered on the basis of the Bulletin Order given below. Refer to this bulletin when answering these questions.

<u>BULLETIN ORDER NO. 67</u>

SUBJECT: Procedure for Handling Fire Occurrences

In order that the Fire Department may be notified of all fires, even those that have been extinguished by our own employees, any employee having knowledge of a fire must notify the Station Department Office immediately on telephone extensions D-4177, D-4181, D-4185, or D-4189.

Specific information regarding the fire should include the location of the fire, the approximate distance north or south of the nearest station, and the track designation, line, and division.

In addition, the report should contain information as to the status of the fire and whether our forces have extinguished it or if Fire Department equipment is required.

When all information has been obtained, the Station Supervisor in Charge in the Station Department Office will notify the Desk Trainmaster of the Division involved.

Richard Roe,
Superintendent

1. An employee having knowledge of a fire should FIRST notify the   1._____

   A. Station Department Office
   B. Fire Department
   C. Desk Trainmaster
   D. Station Supervisor

2. If bulletin order number 1 was issued on January 2, bulletins are being issued at the   2._____
   monthly average of

   A. 8   B. 10   C. 12   D. 14

3. It is clear from the bulletin that   3._____

   A. employees are expected to be expert fire fighters
   B. many fires occur on the transit system
   C. train service is usually suspended whenever a fire occurs
   D. some fires are extinguished without the help of the Fire Department

4. From the information furnished in this bulletin, it can be assumed that the   4.____

    A. Station Department office handles a considerable number of telephone calls
    B. Superintendent Investigates the handling of all subway fires
    C. Fire Department is notified only in ease of large fires
    D. employee first having knowledge of the fire must call all 4 extensions

5. The PROBABLE reason for notifying the Fire Department even when the fire has been   5.____
extinguished by a subway employee is because the Fire Department is

    A. a city agency
    B. still responsible to check the fire
    C. concerned with fire prevention
    D. required to clean up after the fire

6. Information about the fire NOT specifically required is   6.____

    A. track   B. time of day   C. station   D. division

Questions 7-10.

DIRECTIONS: Questions 7 through 10 are to be answered on the basis of the paragraph on
fire fighting shown below. When answering these questions, refer to this paragraph.

FIRE FIGHTING

A security officer should remember the cardinal rule that water or soda acid fire extinguishers should not be used on any electrical fire, and apply it in the case of a fire near the
third rail. In addition, security officers should familiarize themselves with all available fire
alarms and fire-fighting equipment within their assigned posts. Use of the fire alarm should
bring responding Fire Department apparatus quickly to the scene. Familiarity with the fire-
fighting equipment near his post would help in putting out incipient fires. Any man calling for
the Fire Department should remain outside so that he can direct the Fire Department to the
fire. As soon as possible thereafter, the special inspection desk must be notified, and a complete written report of the fire, no matter how small, must be submitted to this office. The
security officer must give the exact time and place it started, who discovered it, how it was
extinguished, the damage done, cause of same, list of any injured persons with the extent of
their injuries, and the name of the Fire Chief in charge. All defects noticed by the security
officer concerning the fire alarm or any fire-fighting equipment must be reported to the special
inspection department.

7. It would be PROPER to use water to put out a fire in a(n)   7.____

    A. electric motor   B. electric switch box
    C. waste paper trash can   D. electric generator

8. After calling the Fire Department from a street box to report a fire, the security officer   8.____
should then

    A. return to the fire and help put it out
    B. stay outside and direct the Fire Department to the fire
    C. find a phone and call his boss
    D. write out a report for the special inspection desk

9. A security officer is required to submit a complete written report of a fire   9.____

     A. two weeks after the fire
     B. the day following the fire
     C. as soon as possible
     D. at his convenience

10. In his report of a fire, it is NOT necessary for the security officer to state   10.____

     A. time and place of the fire
     B. who discovered the fire
     C. the names of persons injured
     D. quantity of Fire Department equipment used

Questions 11-16.

DIRECTIONS: Questions 11 through 16 are to be answered on the basis of the Notice given below. Refer to this Notice in answering these questions.

NOTICE

Your attention is called to Route Request Buttons that are installed on all new type Interlocking Home Signals where there is a choice of route in the midtown area. The route request button is to be operated by the motorman when the home signal is at danger and no call-on is displayed or when improper route is displayed.

To operate, the motorman will press the button for the desiredroute as indicated under each button; a light will then go on over the buttons to inform the motorman that his request has been registered in the tower.

If the towerman desires to give the motorman a route other than the one he selected, the towerman will cancel out the light over the route selection buttons. The motorman will then accept the route given.

If no route or call-on is given, the motorman will sound his whistle for the signal maintainer, secure his train, and call the desk trainmaster.

11. The official titles of the two classes of employee whose actions would MOST frequently   11.____
be affected by the contents of this notice are

     A. motorman and trainmaster
     B. signal maintainer and trainmaster
     C. towerman and motorman
     D. signal maintainer and towerman

12. A motorman should use a route request button when   12.____

     A. the signal indicates proceed on main line
     B. a call-on is displayed
     C. the signal indicates stop
     D. the signal indicates proceed on diverging route

13. The PROPER way to request a route is to

13.____

    A. press the button corresponding to the desired route
    B. press the button a number of times to correspond with the number of the route requested
    C. stop at the signal and blow four short blasts
    D. stop at the signal and telephone the tower

14. The motorman will know that his requested route has been registered in the tower if

14.____

    A. a light comes on over the route request buttons
    B. an acknowledging signal is sounded on the tower horn
    C. the light in the route request button goes dark
    D. the home signal continues to indicate stop

15. Under certain conditions, when stopped at such home signal, the motorman must signal for a signal maintainer and call the desk trainmaster.
Such condition exists when, after standing awhile,

15.____

    A. the towerman continues to give the wrong route
    B. the towerman does not acknowledge the signal
    C. no route or call-on is given
    D. the light over the route request buttons is cancelled out

16. It is clear that route request buttons

16.____

    A. eliminate train delays due to signals at junctions
    B. keep the towerman alert
    C. force motormen and towermen to be more careful
    D. are a more accurate form of communication than the whistle.

Questions 17-22.

DIRECTIONS: Questions 17 through 22 are to be answered on the basis of the instructions for removal of paper given below. Read these instructions carefully before answering these questions.

GENERAL INSTRUCTIONS FOR REMOVAL OF PAPER

When a cleaner's work schedule calls for the bagging of paper, he will remove paper from the waste paper receptacles, bag it, and place the bags at the head end of the platform, where they will be picked up by the work train. He will fill bags with paper to a weight that can be carried without danger of personal injury, as porters are forbidden to drag bags of paper over the platform. Cleaners are responsible that all bags of paper are arranged so as to prevent their falling from the platform to tracks, and so as to not interfere with passenger traffic.

17. A GOOD reason for removing the paper from receptacles and placing it in bags is that bags are more easily

17.____

    A. stored   B. weighed   C. handled   D. emptied

18. The *head end* of a local station platform is the end 18.____

    A. in the direction that trains are running
    B. nearest to which the trains stop
    C. where there is an underpass to the other side
    D. at which the change booth is located

19. The MOST likely reason for having the filled bags placed at the head end of the station rather than at the other end is that 19.____

    A. a special storage space is provided there for them
    B. this end of the platform is farthest from the passengers
    C. most porters' closets are located near the head end
    D. the work train stops at this end to pick them up

20. Limiting the weight to which the bags can be filled is PROBABLY done to 20.____

    A. avoid having too many ripped or broken bags
    B. protect the porter against possible rupture
    C. make sure that all bags are filled fairly evenly
    D. insure that, when stored, the bags will not fall to the track

21. The MOST important reason for not allowing filled bags to be dragged over the platform is that the bags 21.____

    A. could otherwise be loaded too heavily
    B. might leave streaks on the platform
    C. would wear out too quickly
    D. might spill paper on the platform

22. The instructions do NOT hold a porter responsible for a bag of paper which 22.____

    A. is torn due to dragging over a platform
    B. falls on a passenger because it was poorly stacked
    C. falls to the track without being pushed
    D. is ripped open by school children

Questions 23-25.

DIRECTIONS: Questions 23 through 25 are to be answered on the basis of the situation described below. Consider the facts given in this situation when answering these questions.

SITUATION

A new detergent that is to be added to water and the resulting mixture just wiped on any surface has been tested by the station department and appeared to be excellent. However, you notice, after inspecting a large number of stations that your porters have cleaned with this detergent, that the surfaces cleaned are not as clean as they formerly were when the old method was used.

23. The MAIN reason for the station department testing the new detergent in the first place was to make certain that

    A. it was very simple to use
    B. a little bit would go a long way
    C. there was no stronger detergent on the market
    D. it was superior to anything formerly used

23.____

24. The MAIN reason that such a poor cleaning job resulted was MOST likely due to the

    A. porters being lax on the job
    B. detergent not being as good as expected
    C. incorrect amount of water being mixed with the detergent
    D. fact that the surfaces cleaned needed to be scrubbed

24.____

25. The reason for inspecting a number of stations was to

    A. determine whether all porters did the same job
    B. insure that the result of the cleaning job was the same in each location
    C. be certain that the detergent was used in each station inspected
    D. see whether certain surfaces cleaned better than others

25.____

KEY (CORRECT ANSWERS)

1.	A		11.	C
2.	C		12.	C
3.	D		13.	A
4.	A		14.	A
5.	C		15.	C
6.	B		16.	D
7.	C		17.	C
8.	B		18.	A
9.	C		19.	D
10.	D		20.	B

21.	C
22.	D
23.	D
24.	B
25.	B

111

EVALUATING INFORMATION AND EVIDENCE

EXAMINATION SECTION

TEST 1

DIRECTIONS: Each question or incomplete statement is followed by several suggested answers or completions. Select the one that BEST answers the question or completes the statement. *PRINT THE LETTER OF THE CORRECT ANSWER IN THE SPACE AT THE RIGHT.*

Questions 1-9

Questions 1 through 9 measure your ability to (1) determine whether statements say essentially the same thing and (2) determine the evidence needed to make it reasonably certain that a particular conclusion is true.

1. Which of the following pairs of statements say essentially the same thing in two different ways?   1. _____

    I.   Some employees at the water department have fully vested pensions.
         At least one employee at the water department has a pension that is not fully vested.
    II. All swans are white birds.
         A bird that is not white is not a swan.

        A. I only
        B. I and II
        C. II only
        D. Neither I nor II

2. Which of the following pairs of statements say essentially the same thing in two different ways?   2. _____

    I.   If you live in Humboldt County, your property taxes are high.
         If your property taxes are high, you live in Humboldt County.
    II. All the Hutchinsons live in Lindsborg.
         At least some Hutchinsons do not live in Lindsborg.

        A. I only
        B. I and II
        C. II only
        D. Neither I nor II

3. Which of the following pairs of statements say essentially the same thing in two different ways?

   3._____

  I. Although Spike is a friendly dog, he is also one of the most unpopular dogs on the block.
      Although Spike is one of the most unpopular dogs on the block, he is a friendly dog.
  II. Everyone in Precinct 19 is taller than Officer Banks.
      Nobody in Precinct 19 is shorter than Officer Banks.

     A. I only
     B. I and II
     C. II only
     D. Neither I nor II

4. Which of the following pairs of statements say essentially the same thing in two different ways?

   4._____

  I. On Friday, every officer in Precinct 1 is assigned parking duty or crowd control, or both.
      If a Precinct 1 officer has been assigned neither parking duty nor crowd control, it is not Friday.
  II. Because the farmer mowed the hay fields today, his house will have mice tomorrow.
      Whenever the farmer mows his hay fields, his house has mice the next day.

     A. I only
     B. I and II
     C. II only
     D. Neither I nor II

5. <u>Summary of Evidence Collected to Date:</u>

   5._____

  I. Fishing in the Little Pony River is against the law.
  II. Captain Rick caught an 8-inch trout and ate it for dinner.

<u>Prematurely Drawn Conclusion:</u> Captain Rick broke the law.

Which of the following pieces of evidence, if any, would make it *reasonably certain* that the conclusion drawn is true?

     A. Captain Rick caught his trout in the Little Pony River
     B. There is no size limit on trout mentioned in the law
     C. A trout is a species of fish
     D. None of these

6. Summary of Evidence Collected to Date: 6._____

   I. Some of the doctors in the ICU have been sued for malpractice
   II. Some of the doctors in the ICU are pediatricians

Prematurely Drawn Conclusion: Some of the pediatricians in the ICU have never been sued for malpractice

Which of the following pieces of evidence, if any, would make it *reasonably certain* that the conclusion drawn is true?

   A. The number of pediatricians in the ICU is the same as the number of doctors who have been sued for malpractice
   B. The number of pediatricians in the ICU is smaller than the number of doctors who have been sued for malpractice
   C. The number of ICU doctors who have been sued for malpractice is smaller than the number who are pediatricians
   D. None of these

7. Summary of Evidence Collected to Date: 7._____

   I. Along Paseo Boulevard, there are five convenience stores
   II. EZ-Go is east of Pop-a-Shop
   III. Kwik-E-Mart is west of Bob's Market
   IV. The Nightwatch is between EZ-Go and Kwik-E-Mart

Prematurely Drawn Conclusion: Pop-a-Shop is the westernmost convenience store on Paseo Boulevard

Which of the following pieces of evidence, if any, would make it *reasonably certain* that the conclusion drawn is true?

   A. Bob's Market is the easternmost convenience store on Paseo
   B. Kwik-E-Mart is the second store from the west
   C. The Nightwatch is west of the EZ-Go
   D. None of these

8. Summary of Evidence Collected to Date: 8._____

Stark drove home from work at 70 miles an hour and wasn't breaking the law

Prematurely Drawn Conclusion: Stark was either on an interstate highway or in the state of Montana

Which of the following pieces of evidence, if any, would make it *reasonably certain* that the conclusion drawn is true?

   A. There are no interstate highways in Montana
   B. Montana is the only state that allows a speed of 70 miles an hour on roads other than interstate highways
   C. Most states don't allow speed of 70 miles an hour on state highways
   D. None of these

9. <u>Summary of Evidence Collected to Date:</u>   9._____

I. Margaret, owner of *MetroWoman* magazine, signed a contract with each of her salespeople promising an automatic $200 bonus to any employee who sells more than 60 subscriptions in a calendar month
II. Lynn sold 82 subscriptions to *MetroWoman* in the month of December

<u>Prematurely Drawn Conclusion:</u> Lynn received a $200 bonus

Which of the following pieces of evidence, if any, would make it *reasonably certain* that the conclusion drawn is true?

A. Lynn is a salesperson
B. Lynn works for Margaret
C. Margaret offered only $200 regardless of the number of subscriptions sold
D. None of these

Questions 10-14

Questions 10 through 14 refer to Map #3 and measure your ability to orient yourself within a given section of town, neighborhood or particular area. Each of the questions describes a starting point and a destination. Assume that you are driving a car in the area shown on the map accompanying the questions. Use the map as a basis for the shortest way to get from one point to another without breaking the law.

On the map, a street marked by arrows, or by arrows and the words "One Way," indicates one-way travel, and should be assumed to be one-way for the entire length, even when there are breaks or jogs in the street. EXCEPTION: A street that does not have the same name over the full length.

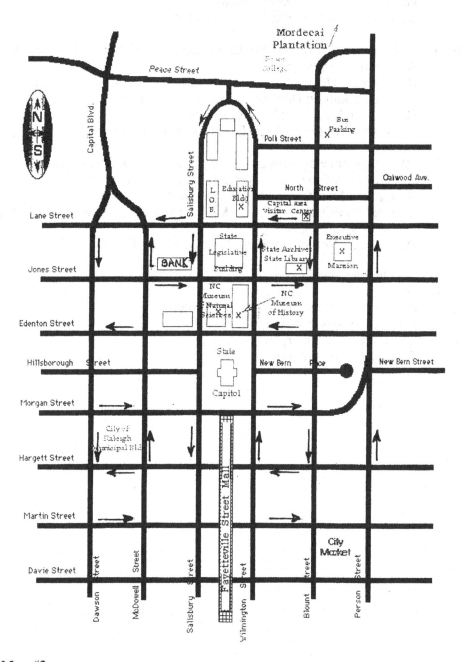

Map #3

10. The shortest legal way from the south end of the Fayetteville Street Mall, at Davie Street, to the city of Raleigh Municipal Building is   10._____
    A. west on Davie, north on McDowell
    B. west on Davie, north on Dawson
    C. east on Davie, north on Wilmington, west on Morgan
    D. east on Davie, north on Wilmington, west on Hargett

11. The shortest legal way from the City Market to the Education Building is   11._____
    A. north on Blount, west on North
    B. north on Person, west on Lane
    C. north on Blount, west on Lane
    D. west on Martin, north on Wilmington

12. The shortest legal way from the Education Building to the State Capitol is   12._____
    A. south on Wilmington
    B. north on Wilmington, west on Peace, south on Capitol, bear west to go south on Dawson, and east on Morgan
    C. west on Lane, south on Salisbury
    D. east on North, south on Blount, west on Edenton

13. The shortest legal way from the State Capitol to Peace College is   13._____
    A. north on Wilmington, jog north, east on Peace
    B. east on Morgan, north on Person, west on Peace
    C. west on Edenton, north on McDowell, north on Capitol Blvd., east on Peace
    D. east on Morgan, north on Blount, west on Peace

14. The shortest legal way from the State Legislative Building to the City Market is   14._____
    A. south on Wilmington, east on Martin
    B. east on Jones, south on Blount
    C. south on Salisbury, east on Davie
    D. east on Lane, south on Blount

Questions 15-19

Questions 15 through 19 refer to Figure #3, on the following page, and measure your ability to understand written descriptions of events. Each question presents a description of an accident or event and asks you which of the five drawings in Figure #3 BEST represents it.

In the drawings, the following symbols are used:

Moving vehicle: Non-moving vehicle:

Pedestrian or bicyclist: ●

The path and direction of travel of a vehicle or pedestrian is indicated by a solid line.

The path and direction of travel of each vehicle or pedestrian directly involved in a collision from the point of impact is indicated by a dotted line.

In the space at the right, print the letter of the drawing that best fits the descriptions written below:

15. A driver headed north on Carson veers to the right and strikes a bicyclist who is also heading north. The bicyclist is thrown from the road. The driver flees north on Carson.   15._____

16. A driver heading south on Carson runs the stop sign and barely misses colliding with an eastbound cyclist. The cyclist swerves to avoid the collision and continues traveling east. The driver swerves to avoid the collision and strikes a car parked in the northbound lane on Carson.   16._____

17. A bicyclist heading west on Stone collides with a pedestrian in the crosswalk, then veers through the intersection and collides with the front of a car parked in the southbound lane on Carson.   17._____

18. A driver traveling south on Carson runs over a bicyclist who has run the stop sign, and then flees south on Carson.   18._____

19. A bicyclist heading west on Stone collides with the rear of a car parked in the westbound lane.   19._____

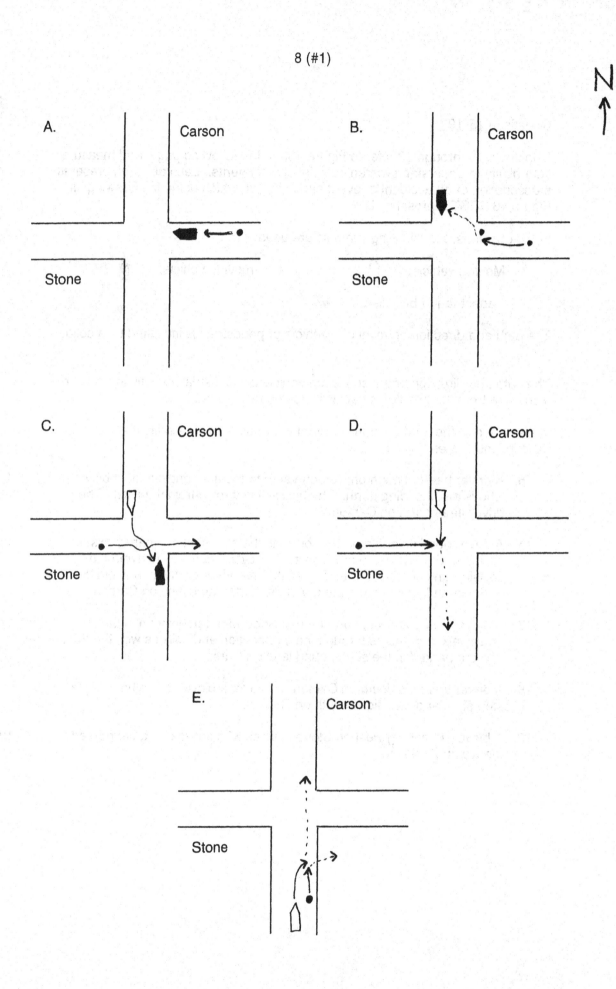

Questions 20-22

In questions 20 through 22, choose the word or phrase CLOSEST in meaning to the word or phrase printed in capital letters.

20. INSOLVENT
    A. bankrupt
    B. vagrant
    C. hazardous
    D. illegal

20._____

21. TENANT
    A. laborer
    B. occupant
    C. owner
    D. creditor

21._____

22. INFRACTION
    A. portion
    B. violation
    C. remark
    D. detour

22._____

Questions 23-25

Questions 23 through 25 measure your ability to do fieldwork-related arithmetic. Each question presents a separate arithmetic problem for you to solve.

23. Officer Jones has served on the police force longer than Smith. Smith has served longer than Moore. Moore has served less time than Jones, and Park has served longer than Jones.
    Which officer has served the longest on the police force?
    A. Jones
    B. Smith
    C. Moore
    D. Park

23._____

24. A car wash has raised the price of an outside-only wash from $4 to $5. The car wash applies the same percentage increase to its inside-and-out wash, which was $10. What is the new cost of the inside-and-out wash?
    A. $8   B. $11   C. $12.50   D. $15

24._____

25. Ron and James, college students, make $10 an hour working at the restaurant. Ron works 13 hours a week and James works 20 hours a week. To make the same amount that Ron earns in a year, James would work about _____ weeks.
    A. 18   B. 27   C. 34   D. 45

25._____

KEY (CORRECT ANSWERS)

1. C	11. B	21. B
2. D	12. C	22. B
3. B	13. A	23. D
4. B	14. B	24. C
5. A	15. E	25. C
6. D	16. C	
7. B	17. B	
8. B	18. D	
9. B	19. A	
10. A	20. A	

SOLUTIONS TO QUESTIONS 1-9

P implies Q = original statement

Not Q implies not P = contrapositive of the original statement. A statement and its contrapositive are logically equivalent.

Q implies P = converse of the original statement.

Not P implies not Q = inverse of the original statement. The converse and inverse of an original statement are logically equivalent.

P implies Q = Not P or Q.

#1. The correct answer is **C**. Item I is wrong because "some employees" means "at least one employee" and possibly "all employees. If it is true that all employees have fully vested pensions, then the second statement is false. Item II is correct because the second statement is the contrapositive of the first statement.

#2. The correct answer is **D**. Item I is wrong because the converse of a statement does not necessarily follow from the original statement. Item II is wrong because statement I implies that there are no Hutchinson family members who live outside Lindsborg.

#3. The correct answer is **B**. Item I is correct because it is composed of the same two compound statements that are simply mentioned in a different order. Item II is correct because if each person is taller than Officer Banks, then there is no person in that precinct who can possibly be shorter than Officer Banks.

#4. The correct answer is **B**. Item I is correct because the second statement is the contrapositive of the first statement. Item II is correct because each statement indicates that mowing the hay fields on a particular day leads to the presence of mice the next day.

#5. The correct answer is **A**. If Captain Rick caught his trout in the Little Pony River, then we can conclude that he was fishing there. Since statement I says that fishing in the Little Pony River is against the law, we conclude that Captain Rick broke the law.

#6. The correct answer is **D**. The number of doctors in each group, whether the same or not, has no bearing on the conclusion. There is nothing in evidence to suggest that the group of doctors sued for malpractice overlaps with the group of doctors that are pediatricians.

#7. The correct answer is **B**. If we are given that Kwik-E-Mart is the second store from the west, then the order of stores, from west to east, is Pop-a - Shop, Kwik- E - Mart, Nightwatch, EZ- GO, and Bob's Market.

#8. The correct answer is **B**. We are given that Stark drove at 70 miles per hour and didn't break the law. If we also know that Montana is the only state that allows a speed of 70 miles per hour, then we can conclude that Stark must have been driving in Montana or else was driving on some interstate.

#9. The correct answer is **B**. The only additional piece of information needed is that Lynn works for Margaret. This will guarantee that Lynn receives the promised $200 bonus.

TEST 2

DIRECTIONS: Each question or incomplete statement is followed by several
suggested answers or completions. Select the one that BEST
answers the question or completes the statement. *PRINT THE
LETTER OF THE CORRECT ANSWER IN THE SPACE AT THE
RIGHT.*

<u>Questions 1-9</u>

Questions 1 through 9 measure your ability to (1) determine whether statements
say essentially the same thing and (2) determine the evidence needed to
make it reasonably certain that a particular conclusion is true.

1. Which of the following pairs of statements say essentially the same thing   1._____
    in two different ways?

    I.   All of the teachers at Slater Middle School are intelligent, but some
    are irrational thinkers.
         Although some teachers at Slater Middle School are irrational
    thinkers, all of them are intelligent.
    II. Nobody has no friends.
         Everybody has at least one friend.

       A. I only
       B. I and II
       C. II only
       D. Neither I nor II

2. Which of the following pairs of statements say essentially the same thing   2._____
    in two different ways?

    I.   Although bananas taste good to most people, they are also a healthy
    food.
         Bananas are a healthy food, but most people eat them because they
    taste good.
    II. If Dr. Jones is in, we should call at the office.
         Either Dr. Jones is in, or we should not call at the office.

       A. I only
       B. I and II
       C. II only
       D. Neither I nor II

124

3. Which of the following pairs of statements say essentially the same thing   3._____
   in two different ways?

   I.   Some millworkers work two shifts.
        If someone works only one shift, he is probably not a millworker.
   II. If a letter carrier clocks in at nine, he can finish his route by the end of
   the day.
        If a letter carrier does not clock in at nine, he cannot finish his route by
   the end of the day.

      A. I only
      B. I and II
      C. II only
      D. Neither I nor II

4. Which of the following pairs of statements say essentially the same thing   4._____
   in two different ways?

   I.   If a member of the swim team attends every practice, he will compete
   in the next meet.
        Either a swim team member will compete in the next meet, or he did
   not attend every practice.
   II. All the engineers in the drafting department who wear glasses know
   how to use AutoCAD.
        If an engineer wears glasses he will know how to use AutoCAD.

      A. I only
      B. I and II
      C. II only
      D. Neither I nor II

5. Summary of Evidence Collected to Date: 5._____

   All of the parents who attend the weekly parenting seminars are high
   school graduates.

   Prematurely Drawn Conclusion: Some parents who attend the weekly
   parenting seminars have been convicted of child abuse.

   Which of the following pieces of evidence, if any, would make it
   reasonably certain that the conclusion drawn is true?

      A. Those convicted of child abuse are often high school graduates
      B. Some high school graduates have been convicted of child abuse
      C. There is no correlation between education level and the incidence
          of child abuse
      D. None of these

6. <u>Summary of Evidence Collected to Date:</u>   6._____

I. Mr. Cantwell promised to vote for new school buses if he was reelected to the board.
II. If the new school buses are approved by the school board, then Mr. Cantwell was not reelected to the board.

<u>Prematurely Drawn Conclusion:</u> Approval of the new school buses was defeated in spite of Mr. Cantwell's vote.

Which of the following pieces of evidence, if any, would make it *reasonably certain* that the conclusion drawn is true?

    A. Mr. Cantwell decided not to run for reelection
    B. Mr. Cantwell was reelected to the board
    C. Mr. Cantwell changed his mind and voted against the new buses
    D. None of these

7. <u>Summary of Evidence Collected to Date:</u>   7._____

I. The station employs three detectives: Francis, White and Stern. One of the detectives is a lieutenant, one is a sergeant and one is a major.
II. Francis is not a lieutenant.

<u>Prematurely Drawn Conclusion:</u> Jackson is a lieutenant.

Which of the following pieces of evidence, if any, would make it *reasonably certain* that the conclusion drawn is true?

    A. Stern is not a sergeant
    B. Stern is a major
    C. Francis is a major
    D. None of these

8. <u>Summary of Evidence Collected to Date:</u>   8._____

I. In the office building, every survival kit that contains a gas mask also contains anthrax vaccine.
II. Some of the kits containing water purification tablets also contain anthrax vaccine.

<u>Prematurely Drawn Conclusion:</u> If the survival kit near the typists' pool contains a gas mask, it does not contain water purification tablets.

Which of the following pieces of evidence, if any, would make it *reasonably certain* that the conclusion drawn is true?

    A. Some survival kits contain all three items
    B. The survival kit near the typists' pool contains anthrax vaccine
    C. The survival kit near the typists' pool contains only two of these items
    D. None of these

9. <u>Summary of Evidence Collected to Date:</u>   9._____

The shrink-wrap mechanism is designed to shut itself off if the heating coil temperature drops below 400° during the twin cycle.

<u>Prematurely Drawn Conclusion:</u> If the machine was operating the twin cycle on Monday, it was not operating properly.

Which of the following pieces of evidence, if any, would make it *reasonably certain* that the conclusion drawn is true?

    A. On Monday the heating coil temperature reached 450°
    B. When the machine performs functions other than the twin cycle, the heating coil temperature sometimes drops below 400°
    C. The shrink-wrap mechanism did not shut itself off on Monday
    D. None of these

Questions 10-14

Questions 10 through 14 refer to Map #4, located on the following page, and measure your ability to orient yourself within a given section of town, neighborhood or particular area. Each of the questions describes a starting point and a destination. Assume that you are driving a car in the area shown on the map accompanying the questions. Use the map as a basis for the shortest way to get from one point to another without breaking the law.

On the map, a street marked by arrows, or by arrows and the words "One Way," indicates one-way travel, and should be assumed to be one-way for the entire length, even when there are breaks or jogs in the street. EXCEPTION: A street that does not have the same name over the full length.

10. The shortest legal way from the State Capitol to Idaho Power is   10._____
    A. south on Capitol Blvd., west on Main, north on 12th
    B. south on 8th, west on Main
    C. west on Jefferson, south on 12th
    D. south on Capitol Blvd., west on Front, north on 12th

11. The shortest legal way from the Jefferson Place Building to the   11._____
Statesman Building is
    A. east on Jefferson, south on Capitol Blvd.
    B. south on 8th, east on Main
    C. east on Jefferson, south on 4th, west on Main
    D. south on 9th, east on Main

12. The shortest legal way from Julia Davis Park to Owyhee Plaza Hotel is   12._____
    A. north on 5th, west on Front, north on 11th
    B. north on 6th, west on Main
    C. west on Battery, north on 9th, west on Front, north on Main
    D. north on 5th, west on Front, north on 13th, east on Main

13. The shortest legal way from the Big Easy to City Hall is   13._____
    A. north on 9th, east on Main
    B. east on Myrtle, north on Capitol Blvd.
    C. north on 9th, east on Idaho
    D. east on Myrtle, north on 6th

14. The shortest legal way from the Boise Contemporary Theater to the   14._____
Pioneer Building is
    A. north on 9th, east on Main
    B. north on 9th, east on Myrtle, north on 6th
    C. east on Fulton, north on Capitol Blvd., east on Main
    D. east on Fulton, north on 6th

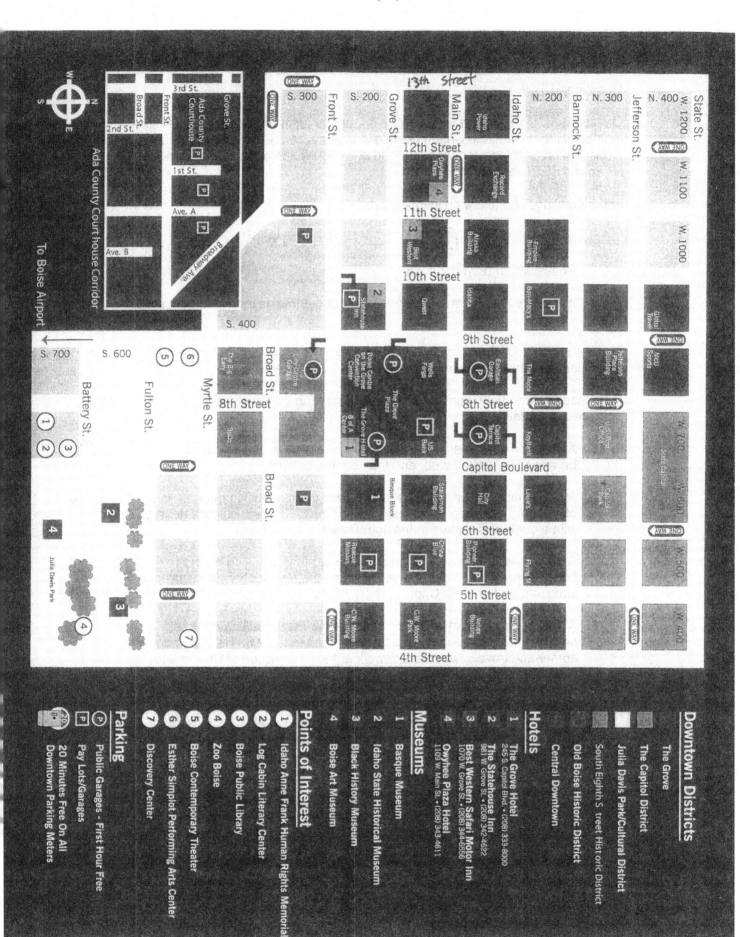

Questions 15-19

Questions 15 through 19 refer to Figure #4, on the following page, and measure your ability to understand written descriptions of events. Each question presents a description of an accident or event and asks you which of the five drawings in Figure #4 BEST represents it.

In the drawings, the following symbols are used:

Moving vehicle: ◻   Non-moving vehicle: ◆

Pedestrian or bicyclist: ●

The path and direction of travel of a vehicle or pedestrian is indicated by a solid line.

The path and direction of travel of each vehicle or pedestrian directly involved in a collision from the point of impact is indicated by a dotted line.

In the space at the right, print the letter of the drawing that best fits the descriptions written below:

15. A driver headed east on Union strikes a car that is pulling out from between two parked cars, and then continues east.

15._____

16. A driver headed north on Post strikes a car that is pulling out from in front of a parked car, then veers into the oncoming lane and collides head-on with a car that is parked in the southbound lane of Post.

16._____

17. A driver headed east on Union strikes a car that is pulling out from between two parked cars, travels through the intersection, and makes a sudden right turn onto Cherry, where he strikes a parked car in the rear.

17._____

18. A driver headed west on Union strikes a car that is pulling out from between two parked cars, and then swerves to the left. He cuts the corner and travels over the sidewalk at the intersection of Cherry and Post, and then strikes a car that is parked in the northbound lane on Post.

18._____

19. A driver headed east on Union strikes a car that is pulling out from between two parked cars, and then swerves to the left. He cuts the corner and travels over the sidewalk at the intersection of Oak and Post, and then flees north on Post.

19._____

FIGURE #4

8 (#2)

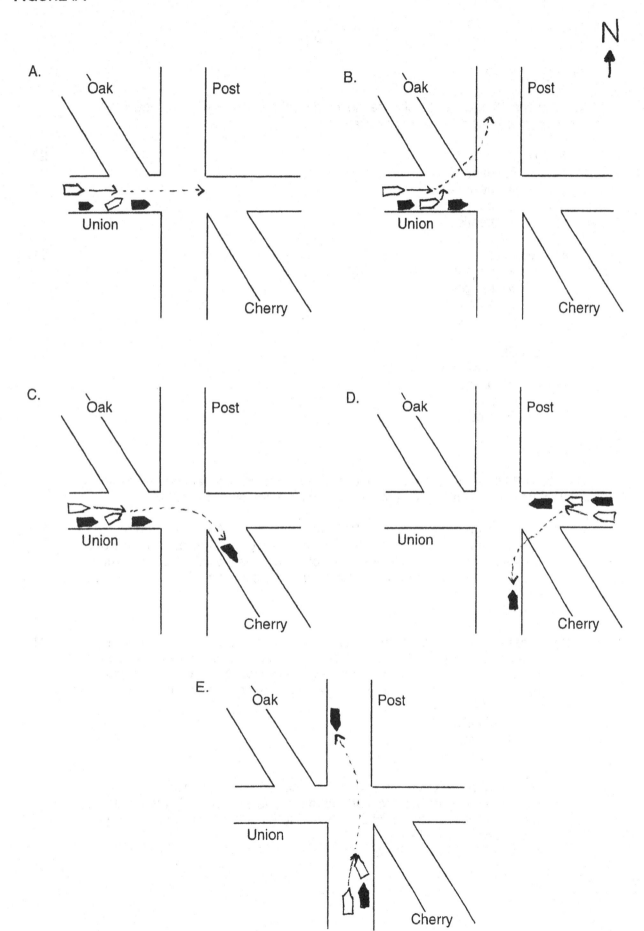

Questions 20-22

In questions 20 through 22, choose the word or phrase CLOSEST in meaning to the word or phrase printed in capital letters.

20. TITLE
    A. danger
    B. ownership
    C. description
    D. treatise

20._____

21. REVOKE
    A. cancel
    B. imagine
    C. solicit
    D. cause

21._____

22. BRIEF
    A. summary
    B. ruling
    C. plea
    D. motion

22._____

Questions 23-25

Questions 23 through 25 measure your ability to do fieldwork-related arithmetic. Each question presents a separate arithmetic problem for you to solve.

23. An investigator plans to drive from his home to Los Angeles, a trip of 2,800 miles. His car has a 24-gallon tank and gets 18 miles to the gallon. If he starts out with a full tank of gasoline, what is the FEWEST number of stops he will have to make for gasoline to complete his trip to Los Angeles?
    A. 4   B. 5   C. 6   D. 7

23._____

24. A caseworker has 24 home visits to schedule for a week. She will visit three homes on Sunday, and on every day that follows she will visit one more home than she visited on the previous day. At the end of the day on _____, the caseworker will have completed all of her home visits.
    A. Wednesday
    B. Thursday
    C. Friday
    D. Saturday

24._____

25. Ms. Langhorn takes a cab from her house to the airport. The cab company charges $3.00 to start the meter and $.50 per mile after that. It's 15 miles from Ms. Langhorn's house to the airport. How much will she have to pay for a cab?
    A. $10.50   B. $11.50   C. $14.00   D. $15.50

25._____

KEY (CORRECT ANSWERS)

1. B	11. D	21. A
2. A	12. A	22. A
3. D	13. B	23. C
4. B	14. C	24. B
5. D	15. A	25. A
6. B	16. E	
7. B	17. C	
8. C	18. D	
9. C	19. B	
10. C	20. B	

SOLUTIONS TO QUESTIONS 1-9

P implies Q = original statement

Not Q implies not P = contrapositive of the original statement. A statement and its contrapositive are logically equivalent.

Q implies P = converse of the original statement.

Not P implies not Q = inverse of the original statement. The converse and inverse of an original statement are logically equivalent.

P implies Q = Not P or Q.

#1. The correct answer is **B**. For item I, the irrational thinking teachers at the Middle School belong the group of all Middle School teachers. Since all teachers at the Middle School are intelligent, this includes the subset of irrational thinkers. For item II, if no one person has no friends, this implies that each person must have at least one friend.

#2. The correct answer is **A**. In item I, both statements state that (a) bananas are healthy and (b) bananas are eaten mainly because they taste good. In item II, the second statement is not equivalent to the first statement. An equivalent statement to the first statement would be "Either Dr. Jones is not in or we should call at the office."

#3. The correct answer is **D**. In item I, given that a person works one shift, we cannot draw any conclusion about whether he/she is a millworker. It is possible that a millworker works one, two, or a number more than two shifts. In item II, the second statement is the inverse of the first statement; they are not logically equivalent.

#4. The correct answer is **B**. In item I, any statement in the form "P implies Q" is equivalent to "Not P or Q." In this case, P = A member of the swim team attends practice, and Q = He will compete in the next meet. In item II, "P implies Q" is equivalent to "all P belongs to Q." In this case, P = Engineer wears glasses, and Q = He will know how to use AutoCAD.

#5. The correct answer is **D**. Because the number of high school graduates is so much larger than the number of convicted child abusers, none of the additional pieces of evidence make it reasonably certain that there are convicted abusers within this group of parents.

#6. The correct answer is **B**. Statement II is equivalent to "If Mr. Cantwell is reelected to the school board, then school buses are not approved. Statement I assures us that Mr. Cantwell will vote for new school buses. The only logical conclusion is that in spite of Mr. Cantwell's reelection to the board and subsequent vote, approval of the buses was still defeated.

#7. The correct answer is **B**. From statement II, we conclude that Francis is either a sergeant or a major. If we also know that Stern is a major, we can deduce that Francis is a sergeant. This means that the third person, Jackson, must be a lieutenant.

#8. The correct answer is **C**. Given that a survival kit contains a gas mask, statement I assures us that it also contains the anthrax vaccine. If the survival kit near the typist pool only contains two items, then we can conclude that the gas mask in this location cannot contain a third item, namely the anthrax vaccine.

#9. The correct answer is **C**. The original statement can be written in "P implies Q" form, where P = The heating coil temperature drops below 400 during the twin cycle, and Q = The mechanism shuts itself off. The contrapositive (which must be true) would be "If the mechanism did not shut itself off, then the heating coil temperature did not drop below 400." We would then conclude that the temperature was too high and therefore the machine did not operate properly.

VISUAL SCANNING

MAP READING

COMMENTARY

This is a test of your ability to orient yourself within a given section or neighborhood of a city or community. In each problem, you are in a vehicle, and you are to choose the shortest way to get from one location to another without breaking any laws. In order to solve each problem, you will need to study the map accompanying each set of four problems. Always begin with the first problem in the set. The starting point for the vehicle in the first problem will be marked by the symbol ▬▶. On the sample map below, the vehicle is heading east on Scott. You will be asked to find your way from the first location to the second location. Each location will be marked with an X. Some of the streets on the map are one-way streets. An arrow ⟹ shows the direction in which you may travel on a street. If there is no arrow, you may travel in either direction. These maps are NOT real. Do not confuse them with any area you may know. Below is a sample problem

SAMPLE QUESTION

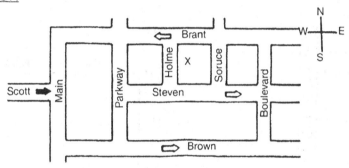

You are on Scott, and you are going to Holme. What is the MOST direct way to get there without breaking the law?
You are on Scott, and you are going to Holme. What is the MOST direct way to get there without breaking the law?

    A.   Go right on Main, left on Brown, left on Boulevard, left on Steven, right on Holme to telephone

    B.   Go left on Main, right on Brant, right on Holme to telephone

    C.   Go right on Main, left on Brown, left on Parkway, right on Steven, left on Holme to telephone

    D.   Go right on Main, left on Brown, left on Boulevard, left on Brant, left on Holme to telephone

The MOST direct way to get from the starting point to the location without breaking the law is described in choice C. Therefore, you would have marked C in the space at the right.

EXAMINATION SECTION
TEST 1

DIRECTIONS: Each map will be followed by several questions. For each question, you will be asked to go from one street to another street. There is ONLY ONE viable selection for each question, although it may not be the shortest route. Any street marked with either a ▬▶ or a ◀▬ is a one-way street.
Unmarked streets are two-ways.
In some cases, a PARTICULAR location on a street is mentioned in the question. This information should be used in arriving at a correct answer. All maps are hypothetical. *PRINT THE LETTER OF THE CORRECT ANSWER IN THE SPACE AT THE RIGHT.*

Questions 1-5.

DIRECTIONS: For Questions 1 to 5, use the following map.

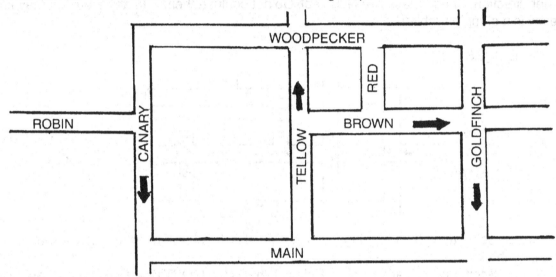

1.   From Brown (east of Red) to Robin.   1.____

    A. Left on Goldfinch, left on Woodpecker, left on Canary, right on Robin
    B. Right on Goldfinch, right on Main, right on Yellow, left on Woodpecker, left on Canary, right on Robin
    C. Right on Goldfinch, right on Main, right on Canary, left on Robin
    D. Right on Goldfinch, left on Main, right on Canary, right on Robin

2.   From Canary to Red.   2.____

    A. Left on Main, left on Goldfinch, left on Woodpecker, left on Red
    B. Left on Main, left on Yellow, left on Woodpecker, right on Red
    C. Left on Main, left on Yellow, right on Brown, left on Red
    D. Right on Main, left on Goldfinch, left on Brown, right on Red

3. From Woodpecker (west of Yellow) to Brown.   3._____

    A.   Left on Canary, left on Main, left on Yellow, right on Robin
    B.   Right on Yellow, left on Brown
    C.   Right on Yellow, left on Main, left on Goldfinch, right on Brown
    D.   Right on Goldfinch, left on Brown

4. From Robin to Goldfinch.   4._____

    A.   Right on Canary, left on Main, left on Goldfinch
    B.   Left on Canary, right on Woodpecker, right on Goldfinch
    C.   Right on Canary, left on Main, left on Yellow, right on Brown, right on Goldfinch
    D.   Right on Canary, left on Main, right on Yellow, left on Brown, left on Goldfinch

5. From Red to Main.   5._____

    A.   Left on Brown, left on Goldfinch, left on Main
    B.   Right on Brown, right on Yellow, left on Woodpecker, right on Canary, left on Main
    C.   Right on Brown, left on Yellow, right on Main
    D.   Left on Brown, right on Goldfinch, right on Main

Questions 6-11.

DIRECTIONS: For Questions 6 to 11, use the following map.

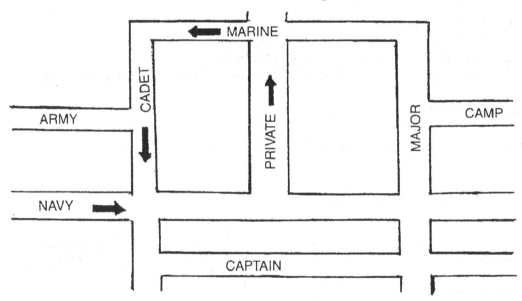

6. From Army to Camp.   6._____

    A.   Right on Cadet, left on Navy, right on Major, right on Camp
    B.   Left on Cadet, left on Marine, right on Major, lelt on Camp
    C.   Right on Cadet, left on Navy, left on Major, right on Camp
    D.   Right on Cadet, right on Navy, left on Major, lelt on Camp

7. From Captain to Marine.   7._____

    A.   Left on Major, left on Marine
    B.   Left on Major, left on Navy, right on Private, left on Marine

    C.   Right on Cadet, right on Marine
    D.   Right on Cadet, right on Navy, left on Private, left on Marine

8.   From Navy (between Private and Major) to Cadet.   8.____

    A.   Right on Major, right on Captain, right on Cadet
    B.   Right on Private, left on Marine, right on Cadet
    C.   Left on Major, left on Marine, left on Cadet
    D.   Right on Captain, right on Navy, right on Cadet

9.   From Navy (west of Cadet) to Array.   9.____

    A.   Left on Private, left on Marine, left on Cadet, right on Army
    B.   Left on Private, right on Marine, right on Army
    C.   Left on Cadet, left on Army
    D.   Right on Major, right on Captain, right on Cadet, left on Army

10.   From Major to Army.   10.____

    A.   Right on Navy, right on Cadet, right on Army
    B.   Right on Captain, right on Cadet, left on Army
    C.   Right on Navy, right on Private, left on Marine left on Cadet, right on Army
    D.   Left on Marine, left on Cadet, right on Army

11.   From Private to Captain.   11.____

    A.   Right on Marine, right on Major, right on Captain
    B.   Left on Navy, left on Major, right on Captain
    C.   Left on Marine, left on Cadet, left on Captain
    D.   Left on Marine, left on Cadet, left on Navy, left on Major, right on Captain

Questions 12-18.

DIRECTIONS: For Questions 12 to 18, use the following map.

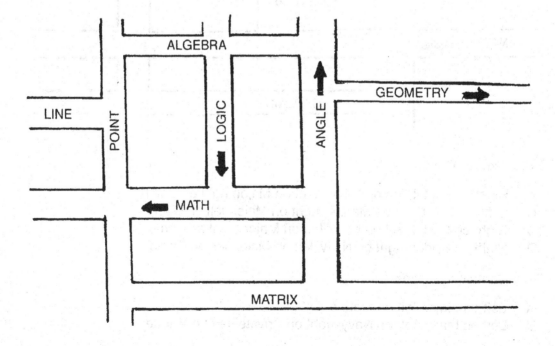

12. From Math to Angle (north of Algebra).   12.____

    A. Left on Point, right on Matrix, left on Angle
    B. Right on Point, right on Algebra, left on Angle
    C. Right on Logic, right on Algebra, left on Angle
    D. Left on Logic, left on Matrix, left on Angle

13. From Algebra to Geometry.   13.____

    A. Left on Logic, left on Math, right on Angle, right on Geometry
    B. Right on Point, left on Matrix, left on Angle, right on Geometry
    C. Left on Logic, right on Math, right on Point, right on Algebra, right on Angle, left on Geometry
    D. Left on Point, left on Matrix, left on Angle, right on Geometry

14. From Line to Logic.   14.____

    A. Left on Point, right on Algebra, right on Logic
    B. Right on Point, left on Math, left on Logic
    C. Left on Point, left on Algebra, right on Logic
    D. Right on Point, left on Matrix, right on Angle, left on Math, right on Logic

15. From Angle (between Math and Algebra) to Point.   15.____

    A. Left on Math, right on Point
    B. Left on Algebra, left on Point
    C. Left on Matrix, right on Point
    D. Left on Logic, right on Math, left on Point

16. From Matrix to Algebra.   16.____

    A. Right on Point, right on Math, left on Angle, left on Algebra
    B. Right on Angle, left on Algebra
    C. Right on Point, right on Algebra
    D. Left on Math, left on Point, right on Algebra

17. From Line to Geometry.   17.____

    A. Left on Point, right on Algebra, right on Angle, left on Geometry
    B. Right on Point, left on Math, left on Angle, right on Geometry
    C. Left on Point, left on Algebra, right on Logic, left on Angle, right on Geometry
    D. Right on Point, left on Matrix, left on Angle, right on Geometry

18. From Logic to Matrix.   18.____

    A. Right on Math, left on Point, left on Matrix
    B. Right on Math, right on Point, right on Matrix
    C. Left on Math, left on Angle, left on Matrix
    D. Right on Algebra, right on Angle, right on Matrix

Questions 19-25.

DIRECTIONS: For Questions 19 to 25, use the following map.

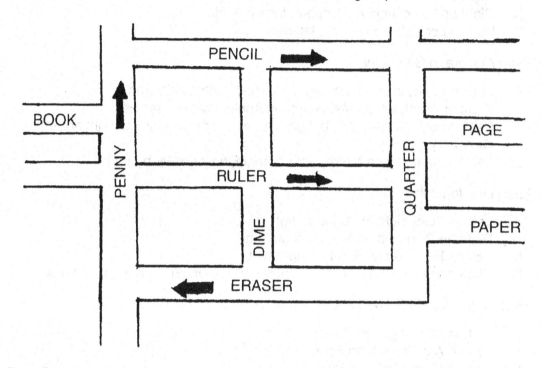

19.   From Page to Dime.   19.____

    A.   Right on Quarter, left on Pencil, left on Dime
    B.   Left on Quarter, right on Ruler, right on Dime
    C.   Right on Quarter, right on Pencil, left on Dime
    D.   Left on Quarter, right on Eraser, right on Dime

20.   From Penny to Eraser (between Dime and Quarter).   20.____

    A.   Right on Pencil, right on Quarter, right on Eraser
    B.   Right on Pencil, right on Dime, right on Eraser
    C.   Right on Ruler, left on Quarter, right on Eraser
    D.   Left on Ruler, right on Dime, right on Eraser

21.   From Book to Quarter (south of Paper).   21.____

    A.   Right on Penny, left on Ruler, right on Quarter
    B.   Left on Penny, right on Ruler, right on Quarter
    C.   Right on Penny, left on Eraser, left on Quarter
    D.   Left on Penny, right on Pencil, right on Quarter

22.   From Paper to Pencil (west of Dime).   22.____

    A.   Right on Quarter, left on Pencil
    B.   Left on Quarter, right on Eraser, right on Penny, right on Pencil
    C.   Right on Quarter, right on Eraser, right on Dime, right on Pencil
    D.   Left on Quarter, right on Eraser, right on Dime, left on Pencil

23. From Pencil (between Dime and Quarter) to Book.   23.____

    A.   Right on Dime, right on Eraser, left on Penny, left on Book
    B.   Right on Quarter, right on Ruler, right on Penny, left on Book
    C.   Right on Quarter, right on Eraser, right on Penny, left on Book
    D.   Right on Dime, right on Ruler, left on Book

24. From Penny (south of Eraser) to Dime (north of Ruler).   24.____

    A.   Right on Ruler, left on Dime
    B.   Right on Ruler, right on Dime
    C.   Right on Pencil, left on Dime
    D.   Right on Pencil, right on Quarter, right on Dime

25. From Ruler (west of Penny) to Paper.   25.____

    A.   Right on Dime, left on Eraser, right on Paper
    B.   Right on Quarter, left on Paper
    C.   Left on Penny, right on Pencil, right on Quarter, right on Paper
    D.   Right on Penny, left on Eraser, left on Quarter, right on Paper

----

KEY (CORRECT ANSWERS)

1.	B		11.	C
2.	C		12.	B
3.	A		13.	D
4.	C		14.	A
5.	D		15.	B
6.	C		16.	C
7.	A		17.	D
8.	C		18.	A
9.	A		19.	D
10.	D		20.	A

21.	D
22.	B
23.	C
24.	A
25.	B

TEST 2

DIRECTIONS: Each map will be followed by several questions. For each question, you will be asked to go from one street to another street. There is ONLY ONE viable selection for each question, although it may not be the shortest route. Any street marked with either a ➡ or a ⬅ is a one-way street. Unmarked streets are two-ways.
In some cases, a PARTICULAR location on a street is mentioned in the question. This information should be used in arriving at a correct answer. All maps are hypothetical. *PRINT THE LETTER OF THE CORRECT ANSWER IN THE SPACE AT THE RIGHT.*

Questions 1-6.

DIRECTIONS: For Questions 1 to 6, use the following map.

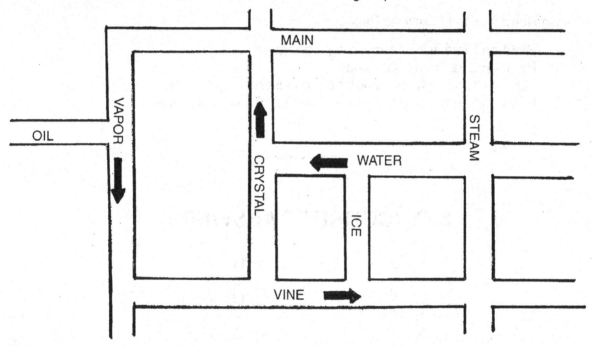

1. From Steam (north of Water) to Ice.   1.____

   A. Right on Water, left on Ice
   B. Right on Water, left on Crystal, left on Vine, left on Ice
   C. Left on Main, left on Crystal, right on Vine, right on Ice
   D. Left on Main, right on Vapor, left on Vine, right on Ice

2. From Oil to Main (east of Crystal).   2.____

   A. Right on Vapor, right on Crystal, left on Main
   B. Left on Vapor, right on Main
   C. Right on Vapor, left on Vine, left on Crystal, right on Main
   D. Left on Vapor, right on Vine, left on Main

3. From Water to Oil. 3.____

   A. Right on Crystal, left on Vapor, right on Oil
   B. Left on Crystal, right on Vine, right on Vapor, left on Oil
   C. Right on Crystal, left on Main, left on Vapor, right on Oil
   D. Left on Ice, right on Vapor, left on Oil

4. From Vine (between Crystal and Ice) to Crystal. 4.____

   A. Left on Ice, right on Steam, left on Crystal
   B. Left on Ice, left on Water, right on Crystal
   C. Left on Ice, right on Water, left on Crystal
   D. Left on Ice, left on Steam, right on Crystal

5. From Main (between Crystal and Steam) to Vine (east of Ice). 5.____

   A. Left on Crystal, left on Vine
   B. Right on Steam, right on Vine
   C. Right on Steam, right on Water, left on Ice, left on Vine
   D. Right on Steam, right on Water, right on Crystal, right on Vine

6. From Ice to Crystal (south of Water). 6.____

   A. Left on Water, left on Crystal
   B. Right on Water, left on Steam, left on Main, left on Crystal
   C. Right on Vine, right on Crystal
   D. Left on Water, right on Crystal, left on Main, left on Vapor, left on Vine, left oh Crystal

Questions 7-12.

DIRECTIONS: For Questions 7 to 12, use the following map.

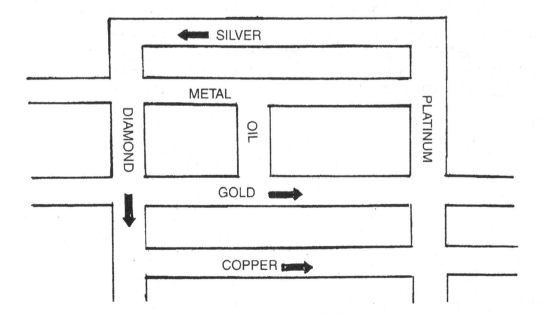

7. From Copper (west of Platinum) to Oil.   7.____

    A. Right on Diamond, right on Metal, right on Oil
    B. Left on Platinum, left on Gold, right on Oil
    C. Right on Diamond, right on Gold, left on Oil
    D. Left on Platinum, left on Metal, left on Oil

8. From Silver to Platinum (south of Copper).   8.____

    A. Left on Diamond, left on Gold, right on Platinum
    B. Left on Diamond, left on Copper, left on Platinum
    C. Right on Metal, left on Platinum
    D. Left on Diamond, left on Gold, left on Platinum

9. From Oil to Diamond (north of Metal).   9.____

    A. Left on Metal, left on Diamond
    B. Right on Gold, right on Diamond
    C. Left on Metal, right on Diamond
    D. Left on Gold, right on Copper, left on Diamond

10. From Platinum (between Gold and Copper) to Gold (between Oil and Diamond) 10.____

    A. Left on Metal, left on Oil, left on Gold
    B. Left on Silver, right on Diamond, right on Gold
    C. Left on Metal, left on Diamond, left on Gold
    D. Left on Silver, left on Oil, right on Gold

11. From Metal (west of Diamond) to Silver.   11.____

    A. Left on Diamond, right on Silver
    B. Left on Platinum, left on Silver
    C. Right on Platinum, right on Silver
    D. Right on Diamond, left on Silver

12. From Diamond (south of Copper) to Diamond (north of Metal).   12.____

    A. Right on Copper, left on Platinum, left on Silver, left on Diamond
    B. Right on Gold, left on Oil, left on Metal, left on Diamond
    C. Right on Copper, left on Platinum, left on Metal, right on Diamond
    D. Right on Copper, left on Platinum, left on Gold, right on Diamond

Questions 13-21.

DIRECTIONS: For Questions 13 to 21, use the following map.

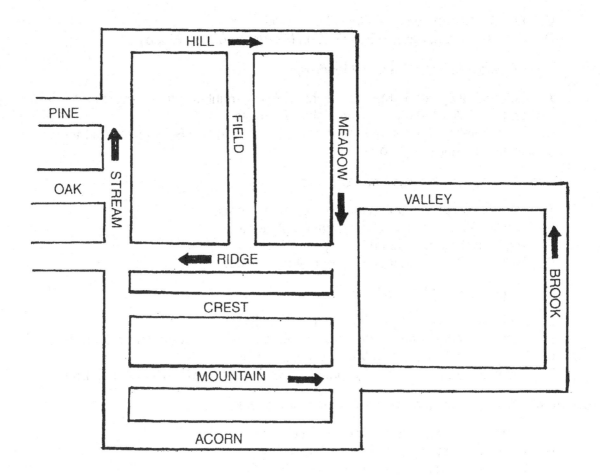

13. From Crest to Field.   13.____

    A.   Left on Meadow, left on Ridge, right on Field
    B.   Right on Stream, right on Hill, left on Field
    C.   Right on Meadow, right on Ridge, left on Field
    D.   Right on Stream, right on Hill, right on Field

14. From Valley to Oak.   14.____

    A.   Left on Meadow, right on Mountain, left on Stream, left on Oak
    B.   Left on Meadow, right on Ridge, right on Stream, left on Oak
    C.   Right on Meadow, left on Hill, left on Stream, right on Oak
    D.   Left on Meadow, left on Crest, right on Stream, left on Oak

15. From Field to Mountain (east of Meadow).   15.____

    A.   Right on Hill, right on Meadow, left on Mountain
    B.   Right on Ridge, right on Stream, left on Mountain
    C.   Left on Ridge, right on Meadow, right on Mountain
    D.   Right on Hill, left on Stream, right on Mountain

16. From Pine to Ridge (east of Field).   16.____

    A.   Left on Stream, right on Hill, right on Field, right on Ridge
    B.   Right on Stream, left on Ridge

C.   Left on Stream, left on Field, left on Ridge
D.   Left on Stream, right on Hill, right on Meadow, right on Ridge

17.   From Brook to Mountain (west of Meadow).

    A.   Left on Valley, left on Meadow, right on Acorn, right on Stream, right on Mountain
    B.   Left on Valley, left on Meadow, right on Mountain
    C.   Left on Valley, right on Meadow, right on Ridge, left on Stream, left on Mountain
    D.   Left on Meadow, right on Mountain

17.____

18.   From Acorn to Meadow (between Crest and Ridge).

    A.   Right on Stream, right on Mountain, left on Meadow
    B.   Left on Stream, left on Crest, right on Meadow
    C.   Right on Stream, right on Hill, right on Meadow
    D.   Right on Stream, right on Crest, right on Meadow

18.____

19.   From Ridge (east of Field) to Brook.

    A.   Right on Meadow, left on Mountain, left on Brook
    B.   Left on Stream, left on Crest, right on Meadow, left on Mountain, left on Brook
    C.   Left on Meadow, right on Valley, right on Brook
    D.   Right on Field, right on Hill, right on Meadow, left on Mountain, left on Brook

19.____

20.   From Meadow (between Crest and Mountain) to Oak.

    A.   Right on Acorn, right on Stream, left on Oak
    B.   Right on Crest, right on Stream, left on Oak
    C.   Right on Mountain, right on Stream, left on Oak
    D.   Left on Hill, left on Stream, right on Oak

20.____

21.   From Acorn to Ridge (west of Field).

    A.   Left on Meadow, left on Ridge
    B.   Right on Mountain, left on Brook, left on Valley, right on Meadow, left on Ridge
    C.   Right on Stream, right on Hill, right on Field, right on Ridge
    D.   Right on Stream, right on Mountain, left on Meadow, left on Ridge

21.____

Questions 22-25.

DIRECTIONS: For Questions 22 to 25, use the following map.

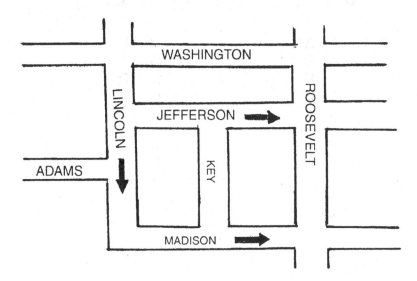

22. From Roosevelt (south of Madison) to Adams.   22._____

   A. Left on Washington, right on Lincoln, right on Adams
   B. Left on Jefferson, left on Lincoln, right on Adams
   C. Left on Washington, left on Lincoln, right on Adams
   D. Right on Jefferson, right on Key, right on Lincoln, left on Adams

23. From Madison (west of Key) to Jefferson (east of Roosevelt).   23._____

   A. Left on Roosevelt, left on Jefferson
   B. Left on Key, right on Jefferson
   C. Left on Key, left on Jefferson
   D. Left on Roosevelt, right on Washington, right on Jefferson

24. From Lincoln (south of Jefferson) to Adams.   24._____

   A. Right on Jefferson, right on Key, right on Madison, left on Adams
   B. Left on Jefferson, left on Lincoln, right on Adams
   C. Left on Washington, right on Lincoln, left on Adams
   D. Left on Madison, left on Roosevelt, left on Washington, left on Lincoln, right on
       Adams

25. From Washington (between Lincoln and Roosevelt) to Key.   25._____

   A. Right on Lincoln, left on Jefferson, right on Key
   B. Right on Roosevelt, right on Jefferson, left on Key
   C. Right on Roosevelt, right on Madison, right on Key
   D. Left on Lincoln, left on Madison, left on Key

KEY (CORRECT ANSWERS)

1.	A		11.	B
2.	C		12.	A
3.	C		13.	D
4.	B		14.	B
5.	C		15.	A
6.	D		16.	D
7.	D		17.	A
8.	A		18.	C
9.	C		19.	D
10.	C		20.	A

21.	C
22.	C
23.	B
24.	D
25.	D

EXAMINATION SECTION
TEST 1

DIRECTIONS: Each question or incomplete statement is followed by several suggested
answers or completions. Select the one that BEST answers the question or
completes the statement. *PRINT THE LETTER OF THE CORRECT ANSWER
IN THE SPACE AT THE RIGHT.*

1. Companies with successful customer service organizations *usually* experience each of   1._____
the following EXCEPT

   A.   fewer customer complaints
   B.   greater response to advertising
   C.   lower marketing costs
   D.   more repeat business

2. To be MOST useful to an organization, feedback received from customers should be   2._____
each of the following EXCEPT

   A.   centered on internal customers
   B.   ongoing
   C.   focused on a limited number of indicators
   D.   available to every employee in the organization

3. Instead of directly saying *no* to a customer, service representatives will usually get BEST   3._____
results with a reply that begins with the words:

   A.   I'll try   B.   I don't believe
   C.   You can   D.   It's not our policy

4. Once a customer problem is identified, each of the following should become a part of the   4._____
service recovery process EXCEPT

   A.   following up on the problem resolution
   B.   making whatever promises are necessary
   C.   providing the customer with what was originally requested
   D.   listening and responding to every complaint given by the customer

5. The percentage of an organization's annual business that involves repeat customers is   5._____
CLOSEST to _____%.

   A.   25   B.   45   C.   65   D.   85

6. Of the following, the _____ is NOT generally considered to be a major source of *service*   6._____
promise.

   A.   customer service representative
   B.   organization
   C.   particular department that delivers product to the customer
   D.   customer

7. A customer appears to be mildly irritated when lodging a complaint. 7.____
   The MOST appropriate action for a service representative to take while attempting resolution is to

   A. allow venting of frustrations
   B. enlist the customer in generating solutions
   C. show emotional neutrality
   D. create calm

8. If an organization loses one customer who normally spends $50 per week, the projected 8.____
   result of reduction in sales for the following year will be APPROXIMATELY

   A. $2600   B. $12,400   C. $124,000   D. $950,000

9. The majority of *service promises* originate from 9.____

   A. organizational management
   B. customer service professionals
   C. the customers' expectations
   D. organizational marketing

10. To arrive at a *fair fix* to a service problem, one should FIRST 10.____

    A. offer an apology for the problem
    B. ask probing questions to understand and confirm the nature of the problem
    C. listen to the customer's description of the problem
    D. determine and implement a solution to the problem

11. Which of the following is NOT generally considered to be a function of *open questioning* 11.____
    when dealing with a customer?

    A. Defining problems
    B. Confirming an order
    C. Getting more information
    D. Establishing customer needs

12. When dealing with a customer, service representatives should generally use the pronoun 12.____

    A. *they,* meaning the company as a whole
    B. *they,* meaning the department to whom the complaint will be referred
    C. *I,* meaning themselves, as representatives of the organization
    D. *we,* meaning themselves and the customer

13. A customer service representative demonstrates product and service knowledge by 13.____

    A. anticipating the changing needs of customers
    B. soliciting feedback from customers about customer service
    C. studying the capabilities of the office computer system
    D. knowing what questions are asked most by customers about a product or service

14. When listening to a customer during a face-to-face meeting, the MOST appropriate non- 14.____
    verbal gesture is

    A. clenched fists
    B. leaning slightly toward the customer
    C. hands casually in pockets
    D. standing with crossed arms

15. Before breaking or bending an existing service rule in order to better serve a customer, a 15.____
    representative should be aware of each of the following EXCEPT the

    A. reason for the rule
    B. location of a written copy of the rule and policy
    C. consequences of not following the rule
    D. situations in which the rule is applicable

16. The LEAST likely reason for a dissatisfied customer's failure to complain about a product 16.____
    or service is that the customer

    A. does not think the complaint will produce the desired results
    B. is unaware of the proper channels through which to voice his/her complaint
    C. does not believe he/she has the time to spend on the complaint
    D. does not believe anyone in the organization really cares about the complaint

17. Most research shows that _____% of what is communicated between people during 17.____
    face-to-face meetings is conveyed through entirely nonverbal cues.

    A. 10   B. 30   C. 50   D. 80

18. When a customer submits a written complaint, the representative should write a 18.____
    response that avoids

    A. addressing every single component of the customer's complaint
    B. a personal tone
    C. the use of a pre-formulated response structure
    D. mentioning future business transactions

19. A customer service representative spends several hours practicing with the various 19.____
    forms and paperwork required by the company for handling customer service situations.
    Which of the following basic areas of learning is the representative trying to improve
    upon?

    A. Interpersonal skills
    B. Product and service knowledge
    C. Customer knowledge
    D. Technical skills

20. If a customer service representative must deal with other members of a service team in 20.____
    order to resolve a problem, the representative should avoid

    A. developing personal relationships
    B. giving others credit for ideas that clearly were not theirs
    C. circumventing uncooperative team members by quietly contacting a superior
    D. involving customers in the resolution of a complaint

21. A customer service representative is willing to help customers promptly.   21.__
    Which of the following service factors is the representative able to demonstrate?

    A. Assurance   B. Responsiveness
    C. Empathy   D. Reliability

22. A service representative begins work in a specialized order entry job and soon learns   22.__
    that many customers call in with orders at the last minute, causing her routine to be
    thrown out of balance and creating stress.
    After studying the ordering patterns of all clients, the MOST effective resolution to the
    problem would be to

    A. mail reminder notices to habitually late customers in advance of typical ordering
       dates to establish lead time
    B. telephone habitually late customers a few days before their typical ordering dates
       to establish lead time
    C. place the orders of habitually late customers in advance, changing them later if
       necessary
    D. establish and enforce a rigid lead-time deadline to create more manageable client
       behavior

23. For BEST results, customer service representatives will improve service by considering   23.__
    themselves to be representative of

    A. the entire organization
    B. the department receiving the complaint
    C. the customer
    D. an adversary of the organization, who will fight along with the customer

24. Of all the customers who stop doing business with organizations, _____ percent do so   24.__
    because of product dissatisfaction.

    A. 15   B. 40   C. 65   D. 80

25. When using the *problem-solving* approach to solve the problem of a dissatisfied cus-   25.__
    tomer, the LAST step should be to

    A. double check for customer satisfaction
    B. identify the customer's expectations
    C. outline a solution or alternatives
    D. take action on the problem

KEY (CORRECT ANSWERS)

1.	B	11.	B
2.	A	12.	C
3.	C	13.	D
4.	B	14.	B
5.	C	15.	B
6.	C	16.	C
7.	B	17.	C
8.	A	18.	C
9.	B	19.	D
10.	C	20.	C

21.	B
22.	B
23.	A
24.	A
25.	A

TEST 2

DIRECTIONS: Each question or incomplete statement is followed by several suggested answers or completions. Select the one that BEST answers the question or completes the statement. *PRINT THE LETTER OF THE CORRECT ANSWER IN THE SPACE AT THE RIGHT.*

1. Of the following, the LEAST likely reason for a customer to telephone an organization or department is to   1.____

    A.   voice an objection   B.   make a statement
    C.   offer praise   D.   ask a question

2. Customer service *usually* requires each of the following EXCEPT   2.____

    A.   product knowledge
    B.   friendliness and approachability
    C.   problem-solving skills
    D.   company/organization knowledge

3. According to research, a typical dissatisfied customer will tell about _____ people how dissatisfied he/she is with an organization's product or service.   3.____

    A.   3   B.   5   C.   10   D.   20

4. When a service target is provided by a manager, it is MOST important for a service representative to know the   4.____

    A.   nature of the customer database associated with the target
    B.   formula for achieving the target
    C.   methods used by other service personnel for achieving the target
    D.   purpose behind the target

5. Typically, customers cause about _____ of the service and product problems they complain about.   5.____

    A.   1/5   B.   1/3   C.   1/2   D.   2/3

6. When a dissatisfied customer complains to a service representative, making a sale is NOT considered to be good service when the   6.____

    A.   customer appreciates being changed to a different service or product
    B.   the original product or service is in need of additional parts or components to be complete
    C.   the customer remains angry about the original complaint
    D.   the original product or service is in need of repair

7. As service representatives, personnel would be LEAST likely to be responsible for   7.____

    A.   service   B.   marketing
    C.   problem-solving   D.   sales

8. When writing a memorandum on a customer complaint, _____ can be considered
optional by a service representative.

    A.   the date the complaint was filed and/or the problem occurred
    B.   a summary of the customer's comments
    C.   the address of the customer
    D.   a suggestion for correcting the situation

8.____

9. In most successful organizations, customer service is considered PRIMARILY to be the
domain of the

    A.   entire organization
    B.   sales department
    C.   complaint department
    D.   service department

9.____

10. According to MOST research, the cost of attracting a new customer, in relation to the
cost of retaining a current customer, is about

    A.   half as much
    B.   about the same
    C.   twice as much
    D.   five times as much

10.____

11. If a customer service representative is unable to do what a customer asks, the representative should avoid

    A.   quoting organizational policy regarding the customer's request
    B.   explaining why it cannot be done
    C.   making specific statements
    D.   offering alternatives

11.____

12. When a customer presents a service representative with a request, the representative's
FIRST reaction should *usually* be a(n)

    A.   apology
    B.   friendly greeting
    C.   statement of organizational policy regarding the request
    D.   request for clarifying information

12.____

13. It is NOT a primary reason for written communication with customers to

    A.   create documentation
    B.   solidify relationships
    C.   confirm understanding
    D.   solicit business contact

13.____

14. Of the following, which would be LEAST frustrating for a customer to hear from a service
representative?

    A.   You will have to
    B.   I will do my best
    C.   Let me see what I can do
    D.   He/she should be back any minute

14.____

15. A customer appears to be mildly irritated when lodging a complaint.
It is MOST appropriate for a service representative to demonstrate _____ in reaction
to the complaint.

    A.   urgency
    B.   empathy
    C.   nonchalance
    D.   surprise

15.____

16. The _____ would be indirectly served by an individual who takes customer orders at an organization's telephone center.

    A. customer   B. management personnel
    C. billing agents   D. warehouse staff

16.____

17. Based on the actions of a customer service representative, customers will be MOST likely to make judgments concerning each of the following EXCEPT the

    A. kind of people employed by the organization
    B. company's value system
    C. organization's commitment to advertised promises
    D. value of the organization's product

17.____

18. When dealing with customers, a service representative's apologies, if necessary, should NOT be

    A. immediate   B. official   C. sincere   D. personal

18.____

19. Of all the customers who stop doing business with organizations, approximately _____ percent do so because of indifferent treatment by employees.

    A. 20   B. 45   C. 70   D. 95

19.____

20. If a customer service representative is aware that the organization is not capable of meeting a customer's expectations, the representative's FIRST responsibility would be to

    A. tell the customer of the organization's inability to comply
    B. shape the customer's expectations to match what the organization is capable of doing for him/her
    C. encourage the customer to believe that the organization can do as he/she asks
    D. make the sale on the organization's product

20.____

21. The following is an example of a *bonus benefit* associated with a product or service: A customer

    A. buys a sporty sedan and finds that its tight turning ratio makes it easy to park
    B. buys bread specifically because he wants to receive a coupon for his next purchase
    C. purchases a car and discovers a strange smell in the upholstery
    D. buys a music audiotape and discovers that there are advertisements at the beginning and end of the tape

21.____

22. Approximately _____ percent of customers who voice complaints with an organization will continue to do business with the organization if the complaint is resolved promptly.

    A. 25   B. 40   C. 75   D. 95

22.____

23. Though necessary, a positive, proactive customer satisfaction policy will USUALLY be restricted by costs and

    A. volume of service problems
    B. limitations of management personnel authority
    C. unreasonable customer demands
    D. limitations of service policy

23.____

24. According to MOST customers, _____ prevents good listening on the part of a service representative when a customer is speaking.   24._____

    A. technological apparatus (e.g. voicemail)
    B. frequent interruptions by other staff or customers
    C. asking unnecessary questions
    D. background noise

25. The ability to provide the promised service or product dependably and accurately may be   25._____
defined as

    A. assurance   B. responsiveness
    C. courtesy   D. reliability

KEY (CORRECT ANSWERS)

1.	C	11.	A
2.	B	12.	D
3.	C	13.	D
4.	D	14.	C
5.	B	15.	A
6.	C	16.	B
7.	B	17.	D
8.	C	18.	B
9.	A	19.	C
10.	D	20.	B

21.	A
22.	D
23.	D
24.	B
25.	D

EXAMINATION SECTION
TEST 1

DIRECTIONS: Each question or incomplete statement is followed by several suggested answers or completions. Select the one that BEST answers the question or completes the statement. *PRINT THE LETTER OF THE CORRECT ANSWER IN THE SPACE AT THE RIGHT.*

1. Public organizations *usually* share each of the following customer-service problems with private organizations EXCEPT

   A. aversion to risk
   B. staff-heaviness
   C. provision of reverse incentives
   D. control-apportionment functions

   1.____

2. A service representative demonstrates interpersonal skills by

   A. identifying a customer's expectations
   B. learning how to use a new office telephone system
   C. studying a competitor's approach to service
   D. anticipating how a customer will react to certain situations

   2.____

3. Of the following, _____ is NOT generally considered to be a common reason for flaws in an organization's customer focus.

   A. commissioned employee compensation
   B. full problem-solving authority for front-line personnel
   C. inadequate hiring practices
   D. specific, case-oriented policy and procedural statements

   3.____

4. According to MOST research, approximately _____ percent of dissatisfied customers will actually complain, or make their dissatisfaction with a product known to the organization.

   A. 5   B. 25   C. 50   D. 75

   4.____

5. Which of the following is an example of an expected benefit associated with a product or service?

   A. Before buying a car, a customer believes she will not have to take the car in for repairs every few months.
   B. A customer in a sporting goods store tells a sales-person exactly what kind of trolling motor will meet the requirements of the lakes the customer wanted to fish.
   C. A supermarket shopper buys a loaf of bread, believing that the bread will remain fresh for a few days.
   D. An airline passenger discovers that the meals served on board are good.

   5.____

6. During a meeting with a service representative, a customer makes an apparently reason-   6.____
able request. However, the representative knows that satisfying the customer's request
will violate a rule that is part of the organization's policy. Although the representative feels
that an exception to the rule should be made in this case, she is not sure whether an
exception can or should be made.
The BEST course of action for the representative would be to

    A.   deny the request and apologize, explaining the company policy
    B.   rely on good judgment and allow the request
    C.   try to steer the customer toward a similar but clearly permissible request
    D.   contact a manager or more experienced peer to handle the request

7. While organizing an effective customer service department, it would be LEAST effective   7.____
to

    A.   create procedures for relaying reasons for complaints to other departments
    B.   set up a clear chain-of-command for handling specific customer complaints
    C.   continually monitor performance of front-line personnel
    D.   give front-line people full authority to resolve all customer dissatisfaction

8. Of the following, _____ is an example of *tangible* service.   8.____

    A.   an interior decorator telling his/her ideas to a potential client
    B.   a salesclerk giving a written cost estimate to a potential buyer
    C.   an automobile salesman telling a showroom customer about a car's performance
    D.   a stockbroker offering investment advice over the telephone

9. As a rule, a customer service representative who handles telephones should always   9.____
answer a call within no more than _____ ring(s).

    A. 1   B. 3   C. 5   D. 8

10. In order to be as useful as possible to an organization, feedback received from custom-   10.____
ers should NOT be

    A.   portrayed on a line graph or similar device
    B.   used to provide a general overview
    C.   focused on end-use customers
    D.   available upon demand

11. Of all the customers who switch to competing organizations, approximately _____ per-   11.____
cent do so because of poor service.

    A. 25   B. 40   C. 75   D. 95

12. When customers offer information that is incorrect in their complaints, a service repre-   12.____
sentative should do each of the following EXCEPT

    A.   assume that the customer is making an innocent mistake
    B.   look for opportunities to educate the customer
    C.   calmly state a reasonable argument that will correct the customer's mistake
    D.   believe the customer until he/she is able to find proof of his/her error

13. In order to insure that a customer feels comfortable in a face-to-face meeting, a service representative should   13.____

    A.   avoid discussing controversial issues
    B.   use personal terms such as *dear* or *friend*
    C.   address the customer by his/her first name
    D.   tell a few jokes

14. Customer satisfaction is MOST effectively measured in terms of   14.____

    A.   cost   B.   benefit
    C.   convenience   D.   value

15. Making a sale is NOT considered good service when   15.____

    A.   there are no alternatives to the subject of the customer's complaint
    B.   when the original product or service is outdated
    C.   an add-n feature will forestall other problems
    D.   the product or service the customer has been using is the wrong product

16. When dealing with an indecisive customer, the service representative should   16.____

    A.   expand available possibilities
    B.   offer a way out of unsatisfying decisions
    C.   ask probing questions for understanding
    D.   steer the customer toward one particular decision

17. Of the following, _____ would NOT be a source of direct organizational service promises.   17.____

    A.   advertising materials
    B.   published organizational policies
    C.   contracts
    D.   the customer's past experience with the organization

18. Generally, the only kind of organization that can validly circumvent the requirements of customer service is one that   18.____

    A.   cannot afford to staff an entire service department
    B.   relies solely on the sale of ten or fewer items per year
    C.   has little or no competition
    D.   serves clients that are separated from consumers

19. When using the problem-solving approach to solve the problem of an upset customer, the service representative should FIRST   19.____

    A.   express respect for the customer
    B.   identify the customer's expectations
    C.   outline a solution or alternatives
    D.   listen to understand the problem

20. During face-to-face meetings with strangers such as service personnel, most North Americans consider a comfortable proximity to be   20.____

    A.   6 inches - 1 foot   B.   8 inches - 1 1/2 feet
    C.   1 1/2-2 feet   D.   2-4 feet

21. When answering phone calls, a service representative should ALWAYS do each of the following EXCEPT

    A. state his/her name
    B. give the name of the organization or department
    C. ask probing questions
    D. offer assistance

21._____

22. If a customer appears to be emotionally neutral when lodging a complaint, it would be MOST appropriate for a service representative to demonstrate _____ in reaction to the complaint.

    A. urgency
    C. nonchalance
    B. empathy
    D. surprise

22._____

23. When soliciting customer feedback, standard practice is to limit the number of questions asked to APPROXIMATELY

    A. 3-5   B. 5-10   C. 10-20   D. 15-40

23._____

24. A customer has purchased an item from a company and has been told that the item will be delivered in two weeks. However, a customer service representative later dis-covers that deliveries are running about three days behind schedule.
The MOST appropriate course of action for the representa-tive would be to

    A. call the customer immediately, apologize for the delay, and await the customer's response
    B. call the customer a few days before delivery is due and explain that the delay is the fault of the delivery company
    C. immediately send out a *loaner* of the ordered item to the customer
    D. wait for the customer to note the delay and contact the organization

24._____

25. Most research shows that _____ % of what is communicated between people during face-to-face meetings is conveyed through words alone.

    A. 10   B. 30   C. 50   D. 80

25._____

KEY (CORRECT ANSWERS)

1.	D		11.	B
2.	D		12.	C
3.	B		13.	A
4.	A		14.	D
5.	B		15.	A
6.	D		16.	B
7.	B		17.	D
8.	B		18.	C
9.	B		19.	A
10.	B		20.	C

21.	C
22.	D
23.	B
24.	A
25.	A

TEST 2

DIRECTIONS: Each question or incomplete statement is followed by several suggested answers or completions. Select the one that BEST answers the question or completes the statement. *PRINT THE LETTER OF THE CORRECT ANSWER IN THE SPACE AT THE RIGHT.*

1. When working cooperatively to identify specific internal service targets, personnel typically encounter each of the following obstacles EXCEPT

    A.   rapidly-changing work environment
    B.   philosphical differences about the nature of service
    C.   specialized knowledge of certain personnel exceeds that of others
    D.   a chain-of-command that isolates the end user

1.____

2. Which of the following is an example of an external customer relationship?

    A.   Baggage clerks to travelers
    B.   Catering staff to flight attendants
    C.   Managers to ticketing agents
    D.   Maintenance workers to ground crew

2.____

3. When a service representative puts a customer's complaint in writing, results will be produced more quickly than if the representative had merely told someone.
Which of the following is NOT generally considered to be a reason for this?

    A.   The complaint can be more easily routed to parties capable of solving the problem.
    B.   Management will understand the problem more clearly.
    C.   The representative can more clearly see the main aspects of the complaint.
    D.   The complaint and response will become a part of a public record.

3.____

4. A customer service representative creates a client file, which contains notes about what particular clients want, need, and expect.
Which of the following basic areas of learning is the representative exercising?

    A.   Interpersonal skills
    B.   Product and service knowledge
    C.   Customer knowledge
    D.   Technical skills

4.____

5. A customer complains that a desired product, which is currently on sale, is needed in at least two weeks, but the company is out of stock and the product will not be available for another four weeks.
Of the following, the BEST example of a service *recovery* on the part of a representative would be to

    A.   apologize for the company's, inability to serve the customer while expressing a wish to deal with the customer in the future
    B.   attempt to steer the customer's interest toward an unrelated product
    C.   offer a comparable model at the usual retail price
    D.   offer a comparable model at the same sale price

5.____

6. Of the following, _____ is NOT generally considered to be a function of closed question-   6._____
ing when dealing with a customer.

    A. understanding requests
    B. getting the customer to agree
    C. clarifying what has been said
    D. summarizing a conversation

7. When dealing with a customer who speaks with a heavy foreign accent, a service repre-   7._____
sentative should NOT

    A. speak loudly
    B. speak slowly
    C. avoid humor or witticism
    D. repeat what has been said

8. If a customer service representative is aware that time will be a factor in the delivery of   8._____
service to a customer, the representative should FIRST

    A. warn the customer that the organization is under time constraints
    B. suggest that the customer return another time
    C. ask the customer to suggest a service deadline
    D. tell the customer when service can reasonably be expected

9. In relation to a customer service representative's view of an organization, the customer's   9._____
view of the company tends to be

    A. more negative   B. more objective
    C. broader in scope   D. less forgiving

10. When asked to define the factors that determine whether they will do business with an   10._____
organization, most customers maintain that _____ is the MOST important.

    A. friendly employees   B. having their needs met
    C. convenience   D. product pricing

11. While a customer is stating her service requirements, a service representative should do   11._____
each of the following EXCEPT

    A. ask questions about complex or unclear information
    B. formulate a response to the customer's remarks
    C. repeat critical information
    D. attempt to roughly outline the customer's main points

12. If a customer service representative must deal with other members of a service team in   12._____
order to resolve a problem, the representative should avoid

    A. conveying every single detail of a problem to others
    B. suggesting deadlines for problem resolution
    C. offering opinions about the source of the problem
    D. explaining the specifics concerning the need for resolution

13. Of the following, the LAST step in the resolution of a service problem should be   13.___

    A. the offer of an apology for the problem
    B. asking probing questions to understand and confirm the nature of the problem
    C. listening to the customer's description of the problem
    D. determining and implementing a solution to the problem

14. _____ is a poor scheduling strategy for a customer service representative.   14.___

    A. Performing the easiest tasks first
    B. Varying work routines
    C. Setting deadlines that will allow some restful work periods
    D. Doing similar jobs at the same time

15. The MOST defensible reason for the avoidance of customer satisfaction guarantees is   15.___

    A. buyer remorse
    B. repeated customer contact
    C. high costs
    D. ability of buyers to take advantage of guarantees

16. A customer service representative demonstrates knowledge and courtesy to customers   16.___
and is able to convey trust, competence, and confidence.
Of the following service factors, the representative is demonstrating

    A. assurance   B. responsiveness
    C. empathy   D. reliability

17. If a service representative is involved in sales, _____ is NOT one of the primary pieces   17.___
of information he/she will need to supply the customer.

    A. cost of product or service
    B. how the product works
    C. how to repair the product
    D. available payment plans

18. A customer appears to be experiencing extreme feelings of anger and frustration when   18.___
lodging a complaint. The MOST appropriate reaction for a service representative to demonstrate is

    A. urgency   B. empathy
    C. nonchalance   D. surprise

19. Of the following obstacles to customer service, _____ is NOT generally considered to   19.___
be unique to public organizations.

    A. ambivalence toward clients
    B. limited competition
    C. a rule-based mission
    D. *clients* who are not really *customers*

20. MOST customers report that the most frustrating aspect of waiting in line for service is   20.____

     A. not knowing how long they will have to wait for service
     B. rudeness on the part of service representatives
     C. being expected to wait for service at all
     D. unfair prioritizing on the part of service representatives

21. Which of the following is an example of an *assumed benefit* associated with a product or   21.____
service?
A customer

     A. buys a sporty sedan and finds that its tight turning ratio makes it easy to park
     B. visits a fast-food restaurant because she is in a hurry to get dinner over with
     C. buys a videotape and believes it will not cause damage to her VCR
     D. tells a salesman that he wants to purchase a high-status automobile

22. On an average, for every complaint received by an organization, there are actually about   22.____
_____ customers who have legitimate problems.

     A. 3   B. 5   C. 15   D. 25

23. Once a customer problem is identified, each of the following should become a part of the   23.____
service recovery process EXCEPT

     A. apologizing
     B. an offer of compensation
     C. empathetic listening
     D. sympathy

24. As a rule, customers who telephone organizations should not be put on hold for any   24.____
longer than

     A. 10 seconds   B. 60 seconds
     C. 5 minutes   D. 10 minutes

25. The LEAST effective way to make customers feel as if they are a part of a service team   25.____
would be to ask them for

     A. information about similar products/services they have used
     B. opinions about how to solve problems
     C. personally contact the department that can best help them
     D. opinions about particular products and services

KEY (CORRECT ANSWERS)

1.	B		11.	B
2.	A		12.	C
3.	D		13.	A
4.	C		14.	A
5.	D		15.	B
6.	A		16.	A
7.	A		17.	C
8.	C		18.	B
9.	C		19.	B
10.	B		20.	A

21. C
22. D
23. D
24. B
25. C

———